William Morris & News from Nowhere

A Vision for Our Time

This book is presented for review by
Seven Hills Book Distributors
49 Central Avenue, Cincinnati, OH 45202
Tel (513)381-3881   Fax (513)381-0753

WILLIAM MORRIS & NEWS FROM NOWHERE
A Vision for Our Time
Edited by Stephen Coleman and Paddy O'Sullivan

Published by Green Books

ISBN 1-870098-37-4 Price: $13.95, Paper

U.S. Pub Date: Available Now

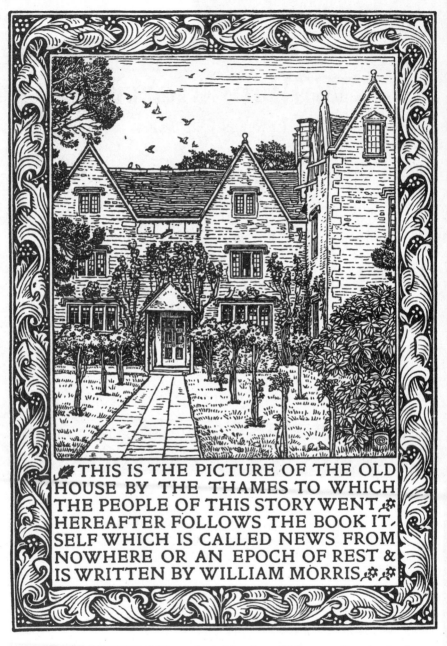

THIS IS THE PICTURE OF THE OLD HOUSE BY THE THAMES TO WHICH THE PEOPLE OF THIS STORY WENT. HEREAFTER FOLLOWS THE BOOK ITSELF WHICH IS CALLED NEWS FROM NOWHERE OR AN EPOCH OF REST & IS WRITTEN BY WILLIAM MORRIS.

The Frontispiece of *News from Nowhere* (Kelmscott Press, 1892) showing Kelmscott Manor.

William Morris
&
News from Nowhere

A Vision for Our Time

EDITED BY
STEPHEN COLEMAN
AND PADDY O'SULLIVAN

GREEN BOOKS

First published in 1990 by
Green Books
Ford House, Hartland
Bideford, Devon EX39 6EE

Photoset in 10 on 13 pt Mergenthaler Sabon
at Five Seasons Press, Madley, Hereford

Printed by Robert Hartnoll Ltd
Victoria Square, Bodmin, Cornwall

Printed on recycled paper

The front cover design (*Honeysuckle*, 1876) by William Morris
is reproduced by courtesy of the Board of Trustees
of the Victoria and Albert Museum

British Library Cataloguing in Publication Data
William Morris & News from Nowhere: a Vision for Our Time.
1. English literature. Morris, William, 1834-1896
I. Coleman, Stephen 1956- II. O'Sullivan, Paddy
828.809

ISBN 1 870098 37 4

ACKNOWLEDGEMENTS

Both editors would like to thank Nicholas Friend, chairman of the working party set up by the William Morris Society to prepare for the centenary of *News from Nowhere*, for his commitment, enthusiasm and continued interest in the production of this book. We are also grateful to our fellow committee members for their support throughout the two years of its production, and to the William Morris Society, for persisting in the task of keeping Morris's work and ideas before the public.

Our own failure to produce a synopsis of Morris's book makes us all the more appreciative of the excellent job done by Clifford Slapper, who took on this task at quite a late stage in the proceedings. Ray Watkinson, besides producing his own chapter, acted as source of information on numerous miscellaneous enquiries about Morris, his circle, and his methods. Finally, we would like to thank John Elford and Satish Kumar at Green Books for their continued support and confidence in this project.

❧ CONTENTS ❧

ᘒ PREFACE ᘓ

The Use of Utopia: History and Imagination

A map of the world which does not include Utopia is not worth glancing at, for it leaves out the one country at which Humanity is always landing.[1]

HUMAN BEINGS POSSESS A UNIQUE CAPACITY to imagine the future. Not only can we sense and think about the circumstances of the present, and reflect upon the past, but we can creatively imagine what we and the generations which come after us are to become. The power of social vision is specifically human: a cat may purr delightedly at a pot of cream, recognizing in its find the most ideal satisfaction; cartoon dogs dream of canine paradises where succulent bones and endlessly cosy surroundings prevail abundantly. The difference between humans and our other animal relations is the human ability to imagine constructively—to convert the sensual dream into conscious aspiration. It is out of such an interplay between dreaming and planning that the utopian imagination emerged. The earliest utopian thinkers tended to be motivated by dreams of physical release from discomfort and oppression. Life was hard; but how might life look if it was easier—or even easy? The imaginative investigations of such alternative ways of living produced the first utopian literature. Too often this juxtaposing of the miserable present with the wonderful time to come is dismissed as idle dreaming. Indeed, some utopian thought has amounted to little more than that. But many utopian visions, including the one under discussion in this book, have comprised more than idle dreams. The utopian imagination, at its most radical, invades the prevailing concept of reality, undermines certainties about what humans must always be like, and casts doubt upon the inevitabilities of the relations of everyday life.

As society has grown older, and systems of organizing life have become more entrenched and seemingly unquestionable, there has been a great need for the utopian submission: 'Let us imagine that life is not as it is, but as it one day might be. Let us inspect the unknown terrain of the future, as if we are about to inhabit it, as if it is an immediate alternative to the fading present.' As the twentieth century comes to an end we need to confront the neurotic obsession to 'face reality'; do anything you like, devise whatever policies you will, but always 'face reality'; like Muslims who must face Mecca thrice daily lest they meet with the most dire of consequences, be sure forever more to 'face reality'. This tyranny of Realism (as if the historical present is somehow more intrinsically real than what has gone or what is to come) is subverted by the utopian who envisages a future which is freed from the apparently unchangeable relationships of the present. The imagined future is a subversive force: the more who imagine a different kind of future, and imagine constructively, materially and determinedly, the more dangerous utopian dreams become. They grow from dreams to aims. Just as the scientist proceeds from speculative hypothesis to practical experimentation, so with social change, what begin as wild dreams, gut feelings, beautiful visions emerge as movements to make the imagined real. 'BE REALISTIC — DEMAND THE IMPOSSIBLE' sloganized the active dreamers who gave the 'realists' a good shock in the Paris of May 1968. A couple of years later John Lennon composed one of the finest modern contributions to utopian literature: the words of *Imagine* urged the millions who sent the song to Number One in the record charts to share the vision of a world without possessions, commerce, countries or religion. 'You may say I'm a dreamer,' sang Lennon, 'but I'm not the only one; I hope some day you'll join us, and the world will live as one.' William Morris (who had little time for music) would have had a lot of time for those words. How well they reflect his own closing words in a lecture delivered in 1883:

> One man with an idea in his head is in danger of being considered a madman; two men with the same idea in common may be foolish, but can hardly be mad; ten men sharing an idea begin to act, a hundred draw attention as fanatics, a thousand and society begins to tremble, a hundred thousand and there is war

abroad, and the cause has victories tangible and real; and why only a hundred thousand? Why not a hundred million and peace upon the earth? You and I who agree together, it is we who have to answer that question.[2]

The enemy of the dreamer of better times to come is the ideologist of the present, armed in defence of the existing miseries with the claim that the prevailing relationships of oppression are immutable. How many rebels have surrendered their visions of great change under the weight of the dogma which insists that There Is No Alternative (the watchword of one leading enemy of radical vision)? Isolation from the mass conformity around us can eventually extinguish hope; the enormous burden of shoving history onwards can demoralize utopian activists, leading us from hope to bitterness. It is easy enough to succumb to the fallacy that there is nothing that can be done to change the world. And yet, look how the world does change. When we began to write this book, the Berlin Wall, the police states of Eastern Europe, the rule of pseudo-socialist tyrants seemed like fixed features of history, entrenched for eternity. Had we been told that within a year these emblems of oppression would be no more, the editors of this book would have laughed—the insecure laughter of those who cannot see what is around the corner. The rapidity of the changes which have occurred since then will serve forever as a warning to those who comfort their conservative minds with assumptions about the grinding, dull, imperceptible slowness of historical change. History can explode. And when it does it is ignited by those who have dared to dream, who have the courage to take on seemingly unbeatable odds, who are brave enough to demand the impossible.

The author of *News from Nowhere* was no idle dreamer. He understood that if a society of comfort, dignity and security was to replace the sordid nightmare of mechanised, regimented, industrial capitalism, so naked in its Victorian splendour for the few at the expense of indecent squalor for the many, then human imagination must be recruited in the struggle for change. Declarations of principles and dry schemes for policy would motivate some people to join the fight, but vision, thought Morris, would be a greater spur. The last words of Morris's book on Socialism (co-written with E. Belfort Bax shortly before *News from Nowhere* was published) makes clear the importance which he attached to the stimulation of the imagination:

> The Socialism which we can foresee and which promises to us the elevation of mankind to a level of intelligent happiness and pleasurable energy unattained as yet, is to us enough of an ideal for our aspirations and as an incentive to our action.[3]

News from Nowhere is Morris's most comprehensive work of utopian vision—an attempt to depict what a socialist society might look like and feel like to be in—but most of Morris's other writings and lectures were replete with appeals to vision. In one lecture on socialism he announced that 'I want to tell you what it is I desire of the Society of the Future, just as if I were going to be reborn into it.'[4] In another talk he stressed the importance of 'being sure that we who call ourselves Socialists understand what we are aiming at . . .'.[5] Lecturing on another occasion he warned that a steadfast movement 'is surely impossible without some high ideal to aim at', for only when guided by such a vision of the end to be achieved will people sacrifice their energies to see it achieved.[6] For Morris, then, vision was not a mere imaginative sideshow intended to amuse the dreamers while the practical revolutionaries were doing the things that mattered. Without vision it would be all too easy to lose sight of what it is that does actually matter. Vision was a means of identifying one's aim—of dressing aims in the costume of desire; vision was a spur to action; and it was a shield against the dangers, implicit in politics, of becoming so preoccupied with the journey that the destiny becomes irrelevant. In this sense, utopian vision should not be regarded as an escape from history into distant, futuristic, wishful thinking. As used by Morris, the utopian imagination served to root wishes, dreams and collective aspirations within the framework of the making of practical history.

As A.L. Morton has pointed out in his masterly work, *The English Utopia*, *News from Nowhere* is the first utopia to have a history. It did not emerge out of nowhere, but is located within the continuity of history: out of class struggle, chronicled in detail, emerged a classless social order. Utopian writers before Morris imagined that their new societies would be brought into being by enlightened thinkers, or by enlightened evolution in the case of Bellamy. Morris's new society had been fought for by people who could only envisage in their imaginations what victory would bring. In the first chapter we are told of a heated debate amongst socialists as to what the future social system will be like. In the following chapters one of them has been transported into the new society. From the comfort of utopia he can look back upon his imaginative vision. From the present the future is explored and from the future the present is remembered. It is this ability to move us through time, making us look upon ourselves as strangers and at strangers as ourselves transformed, which makes for the remarkable greatness of *News from Nowhere*.

STEPHEN COLEMAN

ᴥ INTRODUCTION ᴥ

Who was William Morris?

WILLIAM MORRIS (1834-1896) was one of the foremost designers of his own, or any generation. Of him it has been correctly written that during his lifetime he influenced the appearance of every house in the land.[1] Morris did not, however, confine his activities to design, but was also the owner of a firm which produced a wide range of goods, including stained glass, wallpapers, textiles, carpets, tapestries, furniture, ceramics and paintings. These articles in turn influenced other designers such as William de Morgan and Walter Crane, and a whole generation of other members of the Art Workers' Guild, and the rest of the movement commonly known as the 'Arts and Crafts'. Morris's ideas were also an inspiration to landscape gardeners such as Gertrude Jekyll, and architects such as Walter Gropius of the *Bauhaus*, and through him, the Modern Movement.

If that was not enough, Morris was also, in his day, a successful poet, producing several volumes of both long narrative poems, and shorter pieces. In this, as in most things, Morris was heavily influenced by the Romantic Revival, by the Arthurian legend, and by the art and literature of the Middle Ages, on which, whilst still a young man, he became a noted expert. He was a member of the second generation of artists and writers centred on the Pre-Raphaelite Brotherhood (PRB), founded in 1848 by John Everett Millais, William Holman Hunt, and Dante Gabriel Rossetti. This included several of his life-long friends, notably the painters Cormell ('Crom') Price, Val Prinsep, and especially Edward (later Sir Edward Burne-) Jones.

By the age of forty-three, then, Morris was a successful interior designer, and a noted poet, who, together with his friend the architect Phillip Webb, had also revolutionized British architecture in the design of Red House, near Bexleyheath, London, into which, in 1859, Morris had moved with his new bride, Jane Burden. However, in mid-life, Morris, who until then had shown little interest, became intensely active in politics, joining first the Liberal party, then, in 1883, the Democratic Federation. In 1884, when that organization became the Social Democratic Federation (SDF), he declared himself a socialist, and spent the next eleven years travelling, speaking and writing on behalf of socialism, as well as carrying on his business, and continuing to write poetry.

In 1884, Morris and a number of other activists left the SDF to form the Socialist League, an organization dedicated to revolutionary rather than parliamentarian socialism, which remained Morris's political position for most of the rest of his life. Morris, as well as financing the League, became the editor of its newspaper, *The Commonweal*, in which appeared several of his most famous works, including *News from Nowhere*. In 1887, a parliamentary faction left the League, and in 1890 Morris himself resigned to form the Hammersmith Socialist Society, of which he remained the leading light until his death. In his last years, whilst still an active political speaker, he became interested in printing, founded the Kelmscott Press, and also wrote a series of prose romances set in imaginary heroic societies.

William Morris was born in 1834, into a wealthy middle class family who lived at Walthamstow, Essex. As a boy, he explored Epping Forest, which was then a much more extensive relic of a medieval wood-pasture than it is now. Even then, he was more interested in the medieval world than the modern, and was apparently often to be seen galloping on his pony through the woodland glades, in a child's suit of armour. The principal source of the family income was a set of shares in the Devon Great Consols copper mine near Tavistock in Devon, of which his father, a stockbroker, was a director. These gave Morris an income of £900 a year, of which he was able to make use in his various enterprises throughout his life.

In 1847, at the age of twelve, Morris was sent to Marlborough, which he described as being then 'a new and very rough school'.[2] There, he said, he learned next to nothing, but there was a good library, and he also took time to explore the Marlborough Downs, which are rich in Neolithic and Bronze Age remains, including those of Avebury, Silbury Hill, the Kennett Long Barrows, and the Ridgeway. Thus it was that at Marlborough he began his lifelong fascination for, and relationship with, the past.

In 1853, Morris went up to Oxford to study medieval history. Here he fell under several influences, including those of the High Church Anglicanism of the Oxford movement, at that time very strong in the University, and the Christian Socialism of Charles Kingsley. He later said that the latter would have been a stronger influence earlier in his life had he not soon turned his back on the modern world, and become preoccupied with art, and with the past. Also at Oxford, he befriended Edward Burne-Jones. Together they read poetry, especially Keats; medieval literature, including Mallory and Froissart; and most especially, the works of John Ruskin. From these they learned that they shared the Romantics' revulsion towards Victorian capitalism, their rejection of the replacement of all other values by economic ones, and their preoccupation with the art and religion of the medieval past. They decided to form a brotherhood, perhaps a monastic order, and swore to wage a 'crusade and holy warfare against the age'.[3]

From Carlyle and Ruskin, Morris also obtained ideas which were to serve him well in later life. These were, first, the essential dignity of useful and constructive labour, and second, the role of art in expressing moral judgements about the quality of life in the society in which the artist lives. From Ruskin in particular, he learned of the architectural importance of the great medieval cathedrals of Europe, and of the idea that they are a living record of a nobler and purer society, and a nobler and a purer art, predating the debasement that had taken place under capitalism.

One chapter in Ruskin's *The Stones of Venice*, entitled 'The Nature of Gothic',[4] was their particular inspiration. Under its influence, in the summer of 1855, Burne-Jones and Morris visited northern France, and especially the medieval cities of Amiens, Beauvais, Chartres, and Rouen. Here they studied the architecture of the Gothic, and the magnificent cathedrals that those cities possess. On the quays of Le Havre, they resolved to dedicate their lives to art.

All these influences conspired to draw the young Morris away from the nineteenth century, and into a dream-world of medieval literature and art. Romanticism had long since despaired of the French Revolution, and had turned away from the modern world. The influence of Keats was particularly strong in this respect. Also, the Gothic revival of architecture, begun by, amongst others, the architect G.E. Street, was in full swing. Morris therefore renounced his commitment to enter holy orders, and resolved first to become an architect, articling himself to Street's office.

Burne-Jones had meanwhile also removed himself to London, and had fallen under the spell of Dante Gabriel Rossetti, one of the founder members of the literary and artistic movement, the Pre-Raphaelite Brotherhood (PRB). Under Rossetti's influence, Morris also gave up architecture, and tried his hand instead at painting. In 1857, Rossetti received a commission to decorate, with frescos, the walls of the debating hall (now the library) in the new Oxford Union, and he, Morris, Burne-Jones and others of the group, set off for Oxford. Owing to their ignorance of medieval technique, the paintings soon began to fade, and the work was never finished, but whilst in Oxford again, Morris met Jane Burden, whom he eventually married.

He had also begun to write poetry, which he found much easier to produce than paintings, and in 1858 published his first volume, *The Defence of Guenevere*, based on medieval themes, including the Arthurian legend. At the time, these poems were not received with much acclaim, but some modern authors, e.g. E.P. Thompson,[5] who describes them as among the last true and uncorrupted works of the Romantic Revolt, find them more vigorous and less contrived than Morris's later poetic works. Thus, *Summer Dawn*:

> Pray but one prayer for me 'twixt thy closed lips,
> Think but one thought of me up in the stars.
> The summer night waneth, the morning light slips,
> Faint and grey 'twixt the leaves of aspen, betwixt the cloud bars
> That are patiently waiting there for the dawn:
> Patient and colourless, though Heaven's gold
> Waits to float through them along with the sun.
> Far out in the meadows, above the young corn,
> The heavy elms wait, and restless and cold

The uneasy wind rises; the roses are dun;
Through the long twilight they pray for the dawn,
Round the lone house in the midst of the corn.
Speak but one word to me over the corn,
Over the tender, bow'd locks of the corn.

In 1859, Morris and Jane were married, and moved into their new home, Red House near Bexleyheath, now in south east London. Morris had been unable to find a house in which he had been willing to live, and so commissioned a friend, the architect Phillip Webb, to design him one. The house, with its echoes of the medieval manor house, its use of local brick, its high-pitched gables, its round windows, and its distinctive interior, revolutionized Victorian design, and marked the beginning of modern architecture in Britain.

Red House is generally accredited to Webb and Morris, but according to Marsh,[6] Jane Morris also participated fully in its building, especially its interior and its decoration, herself designing and executing much of the material employed. This was entirely necessary, because, having built their house, the couple, especially Morris, were then unable to find any articles with which they were prepared to furnish it. Consequently, in 1861 was founded 'The Firm'—known first as Morris, Marshall, Faulkner & Co, and later (1874), simply Morris & Co.

The Firm's advertising material stated that it would undertake to produce articles of high quality in the shape of furniture, carpets, tapestries, fabrics, wallpapers, table-glass, stained glass, tiles, ceramics, metal-work (including jewellery), and paintings. Morris enlisted his friends, and other members of the Brotherhood and its circle, such as Burne-Jones, Rossetti, and Ford Madox Brown, to provide designs. Thus at its outset The Firm was able to call on some of the finest artists of the nineteenth century. Morris insisted on authenticity, and would use only natural materials and dyes, and traditional techniques. At the Great Exhibition of 1862, attempts were made to disqualify The Firm's contributions, on the grounds that they were genuine medieval artefacts, retouched![7]

Where he could find people to teach him old techniques, Morris set about learning them. Where they had been lost, he reinvented them. He then taught them to his work force, some of whom became great experts in their own right. In The Firm, Ruskin's ideas about the dignity of labour, of combining brain and manual work, and of performing the manufacturing task from beginning to end, were put into practice. Morris also believed in taking the first applicant for any vacancy, on the grounds that any human being was capable of works of ingenuity and beauty. The Firm's work and products certainly support this view. Unfortunately, they were very expensive, and only well-off people could afford them. Instead of his designs raising the general level of taste, and forcing the producers of shoddy goods out of business, other manufacturers copied Morris's products, but at an inferior standard. This annoyed him, but he was powerless to stop it.

Morris and Jane produced two daughters, Jane Alice (called Jenny), born 1861, and Mary (called May), born 1862. In 1865 they left Red House, to live 'over the shop' at Queen's Square. In 1868, Morris at last received recognition as a poet, with the publication of Parts 1 and 2 of *The Earthly Paradise*. This is a long narrative poem (Parts 3 and 4 were published in 1870) reworking many of the world's great legends. It was enormously successful with the very people whose taste in art and literature Morris despised, the English middle class, so much so that twenty years later, even though he usually styled himself 'William Morris—Designer', newspapers and cartoonists still described him as the author of *The Earthly Paradise*.

According to Thompson,[8] the poem is a sign that Morris had now fully turned his back on the world. Despite its success, he considers it the 'poetry of despair', and a sign that Morris had lost his sense of purpose, and above all, hope. Lindsay,[9] however, believes that writing the poem provided Morris with great solace after the move from Red House, and the deterioration of his relationship with Jane.

About this time, Morris became deeply interested in the legends and sagas of the North, especially those of Iceland. In 1869 he had published a translation, with an Icelander, Eiríkir Magnússon, of *The Story of Grettir the Strong*. Now, in 1871, and again in 1873, Morris visited Iceland, and many of the places mentioned in the sagas. Even today Iceland is, of course, a place where oral tradition is strong, and where people can still recite their genealogy back to the original Norse colonization. This period of Morris's life ends with the publication of *Sigurd the Volsung*, a narrative poem based on, but not translated from, the *Volsunga Saga*, but the effect of Norse decorative ideas upon his own designs persisted to the end.

Also in 1871, Morris and Rossetti took the joint tenancy of Kelmscott Manor in Oxfordshire, a Jacobean Manor house built of Cotswold stone, a few miles from Lechlade on the Thames. No sooner had he arranged this, however, than he left for Iceland, leaving his family and Rossetti behind. Early biographers of Morris (e.g. Mackail,[10] or Vallance[11]) tend to regard this as perfectly normal behaviour, but more recently, Marsh has suggested that the reason for Morris's absence, and Jane and Rossetti's habitation of Kelmscott, is so that they could pursue their love affair, which had begun some years before (1868).[12]

If so, then Morris comes out of this event considerably to the credit, especially when one considers what would have been the effect upon the 'reputation' of Mrs Morris, of the revelation of her adultery to hypocritical Victorian society. The double standards of the time would have allowed both Morris *and* Rossetti to emerge from any scandal completely unscathed, with Morris as the 'wronged' or innocent party, and Rossetti as the vile but glamourous seducer, whereas Jane would, of course, have been completely 'ruined', especially considering her lowly social origins. It was to avoid precisely such a scandal that Morris departed for Iceland, leaving his wife and her lover to spend the summer together, far from any gossip or the likelihood of discovery. That the affair between Jane and Rossetti caused Morris great pain seems fairly clear. The poems from this part of his life (*The Earthly Paradise, The Life and Death of Jason* (1867), *Love is Enough* (1873), are, according to Thompson,[13] full of despair. Also he began, but never published the *Novel on Blue Paper*,[14] which deals with the subject of two men—great friends—in love with the same woman. Iceland provided some comfort, and considerable inspiration ('hatred of lies, scorn of riches, contempt of death, faith in the fair fame won by steadfast endurance, honourable love of a woman'[15]), but in 1876 Morris finally turned his attention to the contemporary world. He never neglected The Firm, or forgot the importance of the past—indeed once he had begun to analyse the present, history became an even stronger source of inspiration, but from 1877 until the deterioration of his health in 1891, the main activity in Morris's life was politics.

At first Morris was a member of the Liberal party, and an admirer of Gladstone. His first political speech was made at the St. James's Hall, London, on 8th December 1876, on the subject of the 'Eastern Question'. Disraeli, the Tory prime minister of the day, wanted to take Britain to war against the Tsarist empire, ostensibly in support of the equally corrupt and autocratic Ottoman Turks, but in fact merely in order to keep control for British capitalism of the Suez Canal. Morris's political naïvety at the time is graphically illustrated by the fact that he was incensed by this hypocrisy on the part of a leading politician, and he wrote not only a ballad entitled *Wake, London Lads*, to be sung at the meeting, but he also published an open letter *To the Working Men of England*, exhorting them not to fight, and not to be duped by any appeals to a spurious patriotism. Its sentiments still spoke volumes at the time of the Falklands War.

To the Working Men of England

Friends and fellow citizens,
There is danger of war; bestir yourselves and face that danger: if you go to sleep, saying we do not understand it, and the danger is far off, you may wake and find the evil fallen upon you, for even now it is at the door . . . We shall pay heavily, and you, friends of the working classes, will pay the heaviest.

And what shall we buy at this price? Will it be glory, and wealth and peace for those that come after us? Alas! no; for these are the gains of a *just* war; but if we wage the *unjust* war that fools and cowards are bidding us wage today, our loss of wealth will buy us loss of hope, our loss of friends and kindred will buy us enemies from father to son.

An unjust war, I say; for do not be deceived! If we go to war with Russia now, it will not be to punish her for her evil deeds done, or to hinder her from evil deeds hereafter, but to put down just insurrection against the thieves and murderers of Turkey; to stir up a faint pleasure in the hearts of the do-nothing fools that cry out without meaning for a 'spirited' foreign policy; to guard our well-beloved rule in India from coward fear of an invasion that may happen a hundred years hence—or never; to exhibit our army and navy once more before the wondering eyes of Europe; to give a little hope to our holders of Turkish bonds:— Working-men of England, which of these things do you think worth starving for, worth dying for? Do all of them rolled into one make that body of *English Interests* we have heard of lately?

And who are they who flaunt in our faces the banner inscribed on one side *English Interests*, and on the other *Russian Misdeeds*? Who are they that are leading us into war? Let us look at these saviours of England's honour, these champions of Poland, these scourges of Russia's iniquities! Do you know them?—Greedy gamblers on the Stock Exchange, idle officers of the army and navy (poor fellows!), worn out mockers of the Clubs, desperate purveyors of exciting war-news for the comfortable breakfast tables of those who have nothing to lose by war, and lastly, in the place of honour, the Tory Rump, that we fools, weary of peace, reason, and justice, chose at the last election to 'represent' us . . .[16]

At about the same time was formed the Society for the Preservation of Ancient Buildings (SPAB), or 'Anti-Scrape' as Morris called it. The Society also contained Carlyle, Ruskin, Burne-Jones, Holman Hunt (one of the original PRB), Webb, and Faulkner, formerly of The Firm. Its purpose was to oppose the insensitive restoration of medieval buildings which at that time was rife, mainly under the auspices of another architect, Sir Gilbert Scott, who had made a fortune out of this activity. Morris was made both Hon. Secretary and Hon. Treasurer. The campaign began with efforts to save Tewkesbury Abbey from just such an episode of vandalism, but soon extended even abroad, for example to St Mark's in Venice.

Morris remained active on the radical wing of the Liberal party for some years, but eventually he resigned, and in 1881 joined the Democratic, later the Social Democratic Federation, led by H. M. Hyndman. In 1883, Morris first read *Das Kapital*. Characteristically, having identified that he should read it, and being unable to obtain an English translation, he read it in French.

It is with Morris's interest in politics, and the 'Anti-Scrape', that began his series of lectures and essays that lasted almost till the end of his life. It has been calculated[17] that between 1877, and his last speaking engagement in January 1896, Morris lectured or spoke at about three political meetings per week, in almost every part of the country. This figure only includes those meetings about which we have knowledge. His subject was almost always the relationship between art and society, art and capitalism, art and socialism. In later years, communism comes to the fore, along with the nature of work in society. This is reflected in the changing nature of the titles of his essays and lectures, for example *The Lesser Arts* (1877), *The Art of the People* (1879), *The Beauty of Life* (1880), *Art and the Beauty of the Earth* (1881), *Art, Wealth and Riches* (1883), *Art and Democracy* (1883), *Useful Work versus Useless Toil* (1884), *Art and Socialism* (1884), *How we live and how we might live* (1884), *The Hopes of Civilization* (1885), *The Dawn of a New Epoch* (1886), *The Ends and the Means* (1886), *The Society of the Future* (1888), *Communism* (1892), *One Socialist Party* (1896).[18] In giving these lectures, Morris was forced to examine his own ideas, and to assess them, in order to explain them, and by that process he was further politicized, made more radical in his opinions, and eventually became a socialist.[19] They therefore give a commentary through time of the development of Morris's ideas, and of his critique of capitalist society.

In *The Lesser Arts*,[20] Morris writes of the tendency for humans to decorate their artefacts, and of how this is something which expresses our essential humanity. Such decorative art is thus the true art of the great mass of people. He then advances a theory that is pure Ruskin— that during the Middle Ages, the distinction between art and craft, which became necessary with the specialization of labour which took place under capitalism, did not exist, and that much medieval 'art', was created by the ordinary people.

> Those treasures of architecture that we study so carefully nowa-days—what are they? how were they made? . . . who was it who designed and ornamented them? The great architect, carefully kept for the purpose, and guarded from the common troubles of common men? By no means. Sometimes, perhaps, it was the monk, the ploughman's brother; oftenest his other brother, the village carpenter, smith, mason, what not—a 'common fellow', whose common everyday labour fashioned works that are to-day

the wonder and despair of many a hard working, cultivated architect. And did he loathe his work? No, it is impossible. I have seen, as most of us have, work done by such men in some out-of-the-way hamlet—work so delicate, so careful, and so inventive that nothing in its way could go further ... no human ingenuity can produce such work as this without pleasure being a third party to the brain that conceived and the hand that fashioned it.[21]

Separation of art from craft under capitalism created a false dichotomy, and elevated some arts—painting, sculpture, music, drama, building design—above the lesser ones, which are mostly the decorative arts—weaving, dyeing, bleaching, interior decoration, fabric and textile design, woodworking, stone carving. But in the ancient buildings of Europe (and other parts of the world?), we see a record of the time when the arts were all one.

At first, Morris thought that the remedy was for the lesser arts to 'come up with' the greater ones, that is, for the standard of design to be so raised that capitalism was no longer able to undermine these lesser arts through the production of 'shoddy', inferior goods. Later, he came to realize that, as in most things, it is never possible to make one change, but only many, and that only a complete social revolution, and a change from a capitalist economy to one based on a broader set of values, would ensure that his *Hopes and Fears for Art*[22] were realized.

In *Useful Work versus Useless Toil*,[23] Morris describes how the need under capitalism to produce surplus value leads to the decline in quality of product and of skill. Both are squeezed in the interests of competition, under which much work has to be devoted to unproductive tasks. Abolition of surplus value would lead not only to better quality goods, but also to improved quality of life.

Developing the economic critique of Marx, Morris's main objection to Victorian society was that the progress and the glory were built on the backs of the poor, the homeless and the oppressed, and at the expense of nature.

... unless people care about carrying on their business without making the world hideous, how can they care about Art?[24]

In this moral stance he was, of course, still strongly influenced by Ruskin. Neither did Morris confine his analysis to European society alone. He realized that colonialism and imperialism not only sucked resources in to the wealthy nations, but were also a means of exporting poverty abroad.

> ... the Indian or Javanese craftsman may no longer ply his craft leisurely, working a few hours a day, in producing a maze of strange beauty on a piece of cloth: a steam engine is set going in Manchester, and that victory over nature and a thousand stubborn difficulties is used for the base work of producing a sort of plaster china-clay and shoddy, and the Asiatic worker, if he is not starved to death outright, as plentifully happens, is driven himself into a factory to lower the wages of his Manchester brother worker, and nothing of character is left him except, most like, an accumulation of fear and hatred of that to him most unaccountable evil, his English master. The South Sea Islander must leave his canoe-carving, his sweet rest, and his graceful dances, and become the slave of a slave: trousers, shoddy, rum, missionary and fatal disease—he must swallow all this civilization in a lump, and neither himself nor we can help him now till social order displaces the hideous tyranny of gambling that has ruined him.[25]

His realization led him to become a socialist at a time when such an act was almost guaranteed to make him a social outcast in some quarters (two of The Firm's most prestigious and lucrative contracts had involved decoration of the interior of St James's Palace), and, according to Marsh,[26] served only further to alienate him from Jane, who, having herself escaped from a life of poverty and deprivation, was not inclined to open her doors to the rest of the working-class.

In December 1884, the Social Democratic Federation split into two. The SDF remained to be dominated by the autocratic Hyndman, whilst Morris and several others, including Marx's daughter Eleanor, her husband Edward Aveling, and E. Belfort Bax, formed the Socialist League. The split was over principles. Hyndman sought to rule the SDF, but the Leaguers were of the view that a socialist body did not require a general-in-chief. The SDF advocated a programme of legislative reforms (the 'Stepping Stones' to socialism), but the League did not have an agenda of palliatives, preferring to stick to the single issue of socialist transformation. The SDF flirted with ideas of state ownership, but the League rejected nationalization, and other statist strategies, as recipes for what it called 'state socialism'.

Thompson[27] describes the affair as being bungled, in that the dissenters actually possessed a majority on the executive of the SDF, but preferred to resign *en masse* once this fact had been established. The reasons for the split were never properly explained to the rank and file of the SDF, the majority of whom might have come the League's way had this been done. Early next year was founded the newspaper of the Socialist League, *The Commonweal*, with Morris as editor, in which appeared many of his most famous works. Amongst the first of these was *The Pilgrims of Hope* (1885), a long narrative poem based on the events of the Paris Commune of 1871, which, at the time, Morris, preoccupied with The Firm, Iceland, Kelmscott, and maybe Jane's infidelity, had scarcely noticed. Perhaps the most famous passage from this poem is 'The Message of the March Wind', part of which we reproduce below.

Like the seed of midwinter, unheeded, unperished.
Like the autumn-sown wheat 'neath the snow lying green,
Like the love that o'ertook us, unawares and uncherished,
Like the babe 'neath thy girdle that groweth unseen,

So the hope of the people now buddeth and groweth—
Rest fadeth before it, and blindness and fear;
It biddeth us learn all the wisdom it knoweth;
It hath found us and held us, and biddeth us hear:

For it beareth the message: 'Rise up on the morrow
And go on your ways toward the doubt and the strife;
Join hope to our hope and blend sorrow with sorrow
And seek for men's love in the short days of life'.

But lo, the old inn, and the lights and the fire,
And the fiddler's old tune and the shuffling of feet;
Soon for us shall be quiet and rest and desire,
And tomorrow's uprising to deeds shall be sweet.[28]

The Pilgrims of Hope was followed in 1886 by *Socialism from the Root Up* (with E. Belfort Bax), and then in the same year, one of Morris's most celebrated works, the romance narrative entitled *A Dream of John Ball*. This consists largely of an imaginary conversation between John Ball, the revolutionary priest from the Peasants' Revolt (1381), and a nineteenth century socialist. In it, Morris illustrates his idea that the struggles of the Middle Ages and those of Victorian England were different, but essentially the same. Thompson[29] calls it 'a meditation on the meaning of history'.

The meaning Morris attributes to history appears to be that it is a continuous struggle between the forces of personal and spiritual liberation, and those of economic and social division and repression. Out of this struggle come developments in society which continuously transform it, sometimes subtly, sometimes on a revolutionary basis. Thus Morris tells John Ball that although his Peasants' Revolt is doomed to failure, by challenging the economic, spiritual and ideological basis of medieval society, it will unleash forces which will lead eventually to the destruction of the old way of life.

Unfortunately, this will lead not to the medieval earthly paradise, but to capitalism. The struggle against this, says Morris, will be far harder and more titanic, and its end much more difficult to bring about. However, as capitalism is an even more vicious form of repression than the feudal system, making the effort to defeat it will be even more important.

Even then, says Morris, the post-capitalist society may not be perfect. It too may be unequal and repressive, or may evolve into such a society. In one of his most famous (and beautiful) statements, Morris says to John Ball

> I pondered how men fight and lose the battle, and the thing they fought for comes about in spite of their defeat, and when it comes turns out not to be what they meant, and other men have to fight for what they meant under another name.[30]

This comment has a moral not only for John Ball, but for all revolutionaries everywhere. It applies equally to events in France in 1789-92, in Russia in 1917-1921, and in Spain between 1936 and 1937, where in all three cases, true popular revolutions, offering the prospect of *real* democracy, were taken over by well-organized and ruthless, but totally unrepresentative authoritarian minorities, and their original aims subverted and overthrown. It explains the appeal of Morris to libertarian communists and anarchists everywhere, even though he himself was not strictly an anarchist, and was strongly opposed to certain trends within anarchist thinking.[31] His socialist vision of a stateless, wageless, moneyless society was very close, however, to that of the anarchist writer, Peter Kropotkin, who was a friend and contemporary.[32]

In 1887 occurred an important but oft-forgotten episode in the history of the socialist movement in England, which became known as Bloody Sunday. During the events surrounding this episode, the right to free assembly was established, although at some cost to life, as the name suggests. Paradoxically, although Bloody Sunday was a victory for the embryonic socialist movement, it represented a considerable defeat for Morris.

The platform of the Socialist League was that it is not possible to transform capitalist society into socialism using parliamentary reform. Neither did they believe in the 'propaganda of the deed' beloved of some of the anarchists then active in London.[33] Instead, Morris and his fellow-Leaguers looked forward to the day when the population as a whole would see the necessity for revolution, and that it would then rapidly come about.

Bloody Sunday was the culmination of a series of clashes between the government, using the police and the army, and the socialist movement, in which, although the right to free assembly was won, the socialists were defeated. Some members of the League had hoped that the widespread social uproar of the time would lead to the revolution, and when it failed to materialize, were disheartened. Several, including Eleanor Marx, broke away, and formed the Bloomsbury Socialist Society, which was dedicated to parliamentary socialism, and which was therefore able to join forces with the Fabian Society and the SDF. At the same time, the League became increasingly under the influence of anarchists.

Morris, however, retained editorship of *The Commonweal*, and in 1890 was published, between January and October, *News from Nowhere, or An Epoch of Rest*, the main subject of this book. He was provoked into writing this by the publication of another utopia, *Looking Backward*, by Edward Bellamy.[34] Morris reviewed this book for *Commonweal*,[35] and although it became immensely popular, he remained extremely critical of it, describing it in his review as a 'cockney paradise'. *Looking Backward* is set in Boston, in the year 2000, and is almost the complete antithesis of *News from Nowhere*. It describes a drab, highly regimented, highly centralized, totalitarian 'state capitalist' society,[36] in which between the ages of twenty-one and forty-five, life consists solely of conscripted physical or intellectual labour (or military service!), beginning with three years of virtual slavery. Work, therefore, instead of being pleasurable, is a regimented obligation. There is strong differentiation between mental and physical labour, and the people who perform these different tasks, and rather than 'to each according to their needs', goods may only be obtained from the State, using a system of labour credit vouchers. In other words, Marx's famous principle is completely reversed—'to each according to their ability'!

The new order depicted by Bellamy in *Looking Backward* did not come about by revolution. Instead, it emerged out of the gradual concentration of capital and resources into the hands of private monopolies. Eventually these merged with what was now the truly 'corporate' state. Rather than depicting a socialist society, *Looking Backward* resembles much more the regimented, totally unfree states which developed in the dictatorships during the first half of the twentieth century, and which have persisted until recently in Eastern Europe, Latin America, and in the People's Republic of China, and which now appear to be developing around the Pacific rim.

In 1890, Morris left the Socialist League, and formed the Hammersmith Socialist Society. Rossetti had died in 1882, and in 1878 the Morris family had moved their town residence to Kelmscott House, Hammersmith. Morris retained the tenancy of Kelmscott Manor, first jointly with his publisher F.S. Ellis, and later on his own. Both houses are mentioned in *News from Nowhere*, which begins at a vastly altered Hammersmith, and ends at Kelmscott Manor.

> ... this many-gabled old house built by the simple 'country-folk' of long-past times, regardless of all the turmoil that was going on in the cities and courts, is lovely still amidst all the beauty

which these latter days have created; and I do not wonder at our friends tending it carefully and making much of it. It seems to me as if it had waited for these happy days, and held in it the gathering crumbs of happiness of the confused and turbulent past . . .[37]

In 1889 Morris attended the Congress of the Second International in Paris, and revisited his beloved Rouen. After Bloody Sunday and the defection of the parliamentary faction from the League, he seems to have been plagued by political doubts, and found himself increasingly isolated politically. In 1890, he had tried to arrange an alliance between the League, the SDF, and the Fabian Society, and even drew up a document which was signed by himself, Hyndman, and George Bernard Shaw for the Fabians,[38] but none of the parties really believed such an accommodation was possible. In 1893, the Independent Labour Party, dedicated to parliamentary reformism was formed, and, owing to the claims it made as to its ability to improve the capitalist system, met with rapid electoral success. Morris acknowledged that perhaps this stage in the struggle for socialism was a necessary one, and that he had been wrong to dismiss such a strategy in the past. This was a pity, as the hundred years since then have shown just how correct Morris was in his scepticism regarding the value of 'socialists' sitting in parliament passing reform legislation.

His last years were marked by two new ventures, both of which he added to his continued running of The Firm, and his political work. The first of these was the establishment, in 1890, of the Kelmscott Press, and the production of a series of fine quality books, including most of his own works, the poems of D. G. Rossetti, editions of Froissart and Mallory, a reprinting of The Nature of Gothic, versions of various medieval texts, culminating, only a few months before his death, in the beautiful Kelmscott Chaucer. Most of these books were illustrated by Morris himself, or by Burne-Jones, and characteristically, Morris took very great pains to find exactly the right inks, and the very best shapes for his typeface. As in all things, in his printing, Morris gave of his uttermost.

The second new venture of his last years was the writing of a series of prose romances, set in imaginary heroic societies. These include

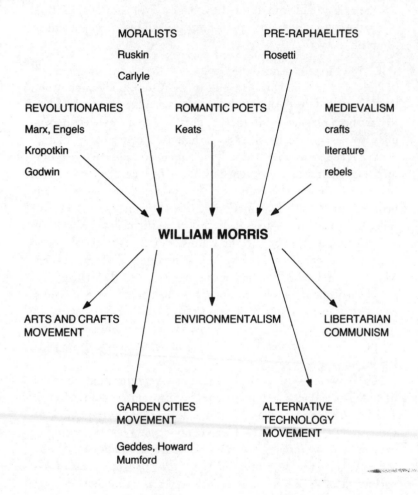

MORALISTS
Ruskin
Carlyle

PRE-RAPHAELITES
Rosetti

REVOLUTIONARIES
Marx, Engels
Kropotkin
Godwin

ROMANTIC POETS
Keats

MEDIEVALISM
crafts
literature
rebels

WILLIAM MORRIS

ARTS AND CRAFTS
MOVEMENT

ENVIRONMENTALISM

LIBERTARIAN
COMMUNISM

GARDEN CITIES
MOVEMENT

Geddes, Howard
Mumford

ALTERNATIVE
TECHNOLOGY
MOVEMENT

Figure 1: The principal influences on William Morris, and his main political and artistic legacy.

The Roots of the Mountains and *The House of the Wolfings* (1889), *The Story of the Glittering Plain* (1891), *The Wood beyond the World* (1894), *The Well at the World's End* (1896), and *The Water of the Wondrous Isles* and *The Sundering Flood* (1897).[39] These were described at the time, by Shaw, as an extraordinary lapse into Pre-Raphaelitism.[40] Thompson,[41] however, suggests that they are not really very Pre-Raphaelite at all, especially with their attitude to the female characters, who can swim, ride and shoot just as well, if not better than the men. Similarly, writes Thompson, the heroes of the prose-romances burst into tears so often that it is a wonder that their armour is not completely rusted!

Scholars have speculated as to the reason for Morris's writing of the late prose-romances, which have variously been described as 'turgid' and 'dream-like'. Thompson[42] suggests that they represent an exploration of the social bond in medieval Germanic society, a somewhat uncharacteristic excursion into the *gemeinschaft* for Morris, and believes also that he wrote them purely for his own enjoyment.

Assessing the contribution of William Morris is not easy, mainly because he attempted, and succeeded at, so much. He serves as a bridge between the Romantics, with their moral revulsion against capitalism, and the Marxist and anarchist revolutionaries of the later nineteenth and early twentieth centuries. Beyond this, however, Morris was a great synthesizer, taking ideas from apparently disparate areas of thought, and producing a totally original analysis of society. His synthesis, in turn, led to further artistic, literary and political movements.

We attempt to explain this in the diagram (Figure 1) where we show the principal influences upon Morris (to which we could add, in his early years, High Church Anglicanism, which led to medievalism, and the Christian Socialism of Charles Kingsley), and his main political and artistic legacy. Besides the Arts and Crafts, Morris also influenced architects of the generation following himself and Webb (e.g. Walter Gropius), landscape gardeners such as Gertrude Jekyll and J.D. Sedding,[43] the town planners of the Garden Cities movement (e.g. Patrick Geddes, Ebenezer Howard, and in North America, Lewis Mumford), anti-statist communists and anarchists, and more recently, the 'green' and the alternative technology movements. As a Romantic, he made the transition to revolutionary socialism, but paradoxically, his greatest contribution may yet lie before him, in that he is by far the most powerful thinker of the last four centuries, in terms of both principles and practice, in the matter of how to organize and maintain a decentralized, collectivized, steady state, ecological society, in which both social responsibility and personal freedom are given equal emphasis, and guaranteed.[44]

In 1891, Morris's health deteriorated. He continued to speak and travel on behalf of socialism, but without the vigour he preferred. In 1895, he went on a cruise to the Norwegian fjords for his health, a journey that ten years before he would have relished, but he was heartily glad to get home. His last public lecture was given in January 1896. On October 3rd, he died. His doctor commented that his death was due to no cause in particular, but mainly to having been William Morris, and done the work, in his lifetime, of ten men.[45]

The coffin was taken to Kelmscott, where Morris was buried in the pouring rain, at Harvest Festival, from a cart bedecked with greenery. Although he had been ill for some time, his death came as a great loss to many socialists and other friends.

> I cannot help thinking that it does not matter what goes into the *Clarion* this week, because William Morris is dead. And what Socialist will care for any other news this week, beyond that one sad fact? He was our best man, and he is dead . . . we have lost him, and great as was his work, he himself was greater. . . . For Morris was not only a genius, he was a man. Strike at him where you will, he rang true. . . . In all England there lives no braver, kinder, honester, cleverer, heartier man than William Morris. He is dead, and we cannot help feeling that for a while that nothing else matters . . . [46]

One Lancashire branch of the SDF speaks for all, however, in the form of the motion passed on hearing of Morris's death:

> Comrade Morris is not dead there is not a socialist living whould belive him dead, for he Lives in the heart of all true men and women still and will do so to the end of time.[47]

PADDY O'SULLIVAN

❧ Synopsis of *News from Nowhere* ❧

CLIFFORD SLAPPER

This is a short chapter-by-chapter summary of News from Nowhere *which is intended to help first time readers of the novel to follow both it and this volume of essays. It is not intended as a substitute for the original.*

Throughout this book, page and chapter references to News from Nowhere *relate to the edition published in* 1973 *by Lawrence & Wishart, London, edited by A. L. Morton.*

The visiting narrator is referred to as Guest, the Guest, or William Guest.

1. DISCUSSION AND BED

At a Socialist League meeting one night, there has been a heated discussion as to what life would be like after a socialist revolution. Afterwards, one of the participants travels home in the discomfort of the underground railway. After a pensive walk by the Thames, he goes to bed and has a restless night.

2. A MORNING BATH

On waking, he is astonished to find that summer weather has arrived, and he goes down to the river to bathe. The waterman, Dick, who takes him out on to the river by boat seems extraordinarily fit, well-presented and courteous. The Thames appears much cleaner, and the buildings along its banks have been transformed. Enquiring about the age of a gloriously beautiful new bridge, he is told that it had been opened in 2003. On offering to pay the waterman, the guest is met with bemused incomprehension: he is providing a service for all who need it, so what would be the point of taking the 'gift' of a crusty old metal token from every passenger? His needs, in turn, are met just as freely as he meets those of others. Dick offers to act as guide, and his friend Bob, a weaver and mathematician from Yorkshire, will take his place on the river.

3. THE GUEST HOUSE AND BREAKFAST WITHIN

In the Guest house, where the 'visitor', William, has spent the night, they are joined by three apparently young women, one of whom, Annie, in fact turns out to be forty-two. We learn that in 1955 there had been a great 'clearing' of housing and a policy of reforestation on the outskirts of London. They enjoy a pleasant but simple breakfast, and are joined by 'Boffin', a dustman clad in a sparkling gold coat, who also writes antiquarian novels. Dick proposes to take William to see his great-grandfather in Bloomsbury.

4. A MARKET BY THE WAY

As they travel through Hammersmith, the visitor is exhilarated by the views of beautiful housing and people's costumes, all in medieval rather than 'modern' style. Their faces are both happy and thoughtful. He asks why there are no poor people to be seen and Dick replies that if people were feeling 'poorly' they would stay indoors.

5. CHILDREN ON THE ROAD

At Kensington they enter some woods, where they find groups of children camping out together. Dick is puzzled by William's reference to 'school': learning has become wholly practical and spontaneous, throughout life. They pass the Houses of Parliament, which now serve as a vegetable market and 'storage place for manure'.

6. A LITTLE SHOPPING

At Piccadilly they find a charming row of pretty shops. William is served with a pipe, tobacco and pouch by two delightful children and is again bewildered by the complete absence of money, buying and selling. When he expresses fears of losing the quite ornate pipe, the girl reassures him that whoever may find it could use it, and he could always get another. An elderly man, who shares part of the ride with them then explains how these booths used to be worked by the descendants of those who used to make others serve them, in order to help cure these descendants of the disease of Idleness.

7. TRAFALGAR SQUARE

They arrive at a transformed Trafalgar Square, which William only just recognizes. Dick becomes exasperated at the thought of the history he has read of the state violence which had taken place there in 1887. It transpires that prisons have been abolished, together with the rest of the machinery of oppression. They then come across some workshops, and some men working on road repairs, whose work is being positively enjoyed, being fully under their control.

8. AN OLD FRIEND

William and Dick arrive at the old British Museum, which William remembers well. The building has been maintained, mainly for fear of damaging the books and other collections if they had to be moved for rebuilding to take place. Dick's great-grandfather mostly lives there, and Dick says that there may be someone else there whom he particularly would like to see himself.

9. CONCERNING LOVE

Dick's great-grandfather, Old Hammond, seems strangely familiar to William. A beautiful young woman, Clara, is also there and goes off to spend some time with Dick. They have lived together previously for two years, and are going to be together again. Old Hammond then explains that divorce courts no longer exist, since quarrels over private property relationships have become a thing of the past. Neither is there any 'unvarying conventional set of rules by which people are judged'. Housekeeping and childbearing are fully respected as vital activities, and men and women live and work happily together in harmony and freedom.

10. QUESTIONS AND ANSWERS

William then asks about education. Old Hammond denounces the destructive indoctrination of the old schooling system, which was born of the poverty it perpetuated. Now no learning is forced, but is always available when sought. He then describes in detail all of the changes that have been made to the urban and rural landscape of London and the rest of the country, with the gradual breaking down of the rigid distinction between country and town.

11. CONCERNING GOVERNMENT

Government, which was just 'the machinery of tyranny', no longer exists at all; the whole people is the 'parliament'.

12. CONCERNING THE ARRANGEMENT OF LIFE

For about one hundred and fifty years, society has flourished without strife and robbery. The end of all private property and class division brought with it the end of all the bitterness and violence it had engendered. Old Hammond explains in detail how this has meant the end of crime and law, and how society now deals with the violent deeds which may still occasionally occur, not with the desire for punishment which is based on fear, but with practical compassion and the avoidance of further damage. Commerce and the market system have also been replaced by a co-operative administration of social affairs.

13. CONCERNING POLITICS

When asked about politics, Old Hammond replies very briefly that they are well off in this regard, as they have none.

14. HOW MATTERS ARE MANAGED

All national boundaries have been abolished, which has allowed a far richer diversity of cultures to flourish. Differences of opinion no longer lead to hostility between permanent political parties. Conflicts are resolved by majority will and, often, through common consensus. There is a system of local Motes, or discussion meetings, with thorough and informed debate leading to democratic decisions on all matters of common interest. Hammond rejects the suggestion that political strife arises from 'human nature', and points out that this true democracy is the only real alternative to tyranny. As for the idea of ending the 'tyranny of society' by every individual enjoying complete independence, this is also rejected as quite impractical.

15. ON THE LACK OF INCENTIVE TO LABOUR IN A COMMUNIST SOCIETY

William asks what special reward there is for hard work, and is told that work has itself become a great pleasure, both as artistic creation, and in the gratification of pleasing others. In contrast to the obsessive and constant cheapening of production standards under the pressures of the old World Market system, work is now geared directly to satisfying human needs in every aspect. There is no longer any reason to produce anything but the very best possible quality for all, and increasing effort is directed towards refining the beauty of all products. If anything, the fear at times is of a shortage of necessary tasks, rather than a surfeit, but such a fear leads only to greater creative embellishment.

16. DINNER IN THE HALL OF THE BLOOMSBURY MARKET
They are rejoined by Dick and Clara and go into a finely decorated dining hall with a number of other people, to eat a simple but exquisitely prepared dinner.

17. HOW THE CHANGE CAME
After eating, William is left alone again with Old Hammond, who explains how the change took place, 'from commercial slavery to freedom'. At the end of the nineteenth century there began a piece-meal and largely ineffective attempt to improve the conditions of the wage-slaves through measures of 'State Socialism', mere legislative palliatives. The real strength, however, lay in the Combined Workers organization which, in the 1950s, carried a Resolution that control of all resources should pass into the hands of the workers. A rally in Trafalgar Square was ruthlessly crushed, but a second meeting there was larger and more difficult to repress with force. A third meeting took place peacefully and food supplies began to be requisitioned by the workers. Under pressure from reactionary commercial people the government put London under military siege. A further Trafalgar Square rally was surrounded by troops, who fired at the crowds and caused a bloody massacre. A Committee of Public Safety representing the producing classes was arrested, but a General Strike secured their release. A period of civil war finally ensued, with workers refusing to supply the reactionary forces, until it became clear that the 'rebels' were wholly triumphant and the old order was dead.

18. THE BEGINNING OF THE NEW LIFE

Hammond then explains how, from that time, people were able to begin to find real joy in one another and in the beauty of life and creative ability.

19. THE DRIVE BACK TO HAMMERSMITH

Dick and Clara return once again, and Old Hammond mentions that he has perhaps been talking to many people besides William, since he may take the story back to those he has come from 'which may bear fruit for them'. On the ride back to Hammersmith, William comments on the colourful and intriguing designs of costume worn by the evening strollers. They decide to get William some fresh clothes for himself.

20. THE HAMMERSMITH GUEST HOUSE AGAIN

They enjoy quite a feast at the Guest House with Boffin, Bob and Annie. After eating they have songs and stories, and William reflects that for the first time he is able to enjoy these pleasures without the nagging irritation of knowing that there is a surrounding social misery or poverty making it possible. He is particularly struck by the disarmingly fresh and frank character of Annie.

21. GOING UP THE RIVER

After a light breakfast and a kiss goodbye from Annie, William takes a boat with Dick and Clara to take part in the hay-harvest upstream.

22. HAMPTON COURT. AND A PRAISER OF PAST TIMES

They stop off for dinner at Hampton Court, then spend a night at Runnymede, at the cottage of an extraordinarily attractive young woman, Ellen, and her grandfather, a 'grumbler' who is dissatisfied with conditions. He praises what he understands of the old ideas of competition, but is countered by William's experience, and by Ellen, who has a strong historical sense and derides his preoccupation with books full of 'dreary introspective nonsense'. After some more songs, they retire for the night.

23. EARLY MORNING BY RUNNYMEDE

There is further discussion with the old 'grumbler', who repeatedly asks the others whether they are sure that they really do like the good conditions which now prevail.

24. UP THE THAMES (THE SECOND DAY)

They continue upstream. Eton has been adapted to become a free centre of real learning, whilst Windsor Castle is now a museum and residential centre. They visit Walter Allen, a friend of Dick's, who explains that a rare tragedy has occurred, in which a man has been killed as a result of a personal conflict. The man responsible is overcome with remorse, and the main fear is that he may now take his own life. Walter agrees to accompany them further up the river, as he wants to make arrangements for this man who has killed to spend some time alone in a house further up, in order to get over his grief and torment peacefully.

25. THE THIRD DAY ON THE THAMES

On the way into Berkshire a group of young girls playing on the grass want the travellers to take breakfast with them, but they move on after some discussion since they want to begin the hay-harvest further up the river.

26. THE OBSTINATE REFUSERS

They come across a group of people who are anxious to complete some building work and therefore do not wish to join in the harvesting. This wish is respected, with some merriment, by the other people in the area.

27. THE UPPER WATERS

They set Walter Allen ashore at Streatley, and at Wallingford they encounter Henry Morsom, an old man who explains in some detail how it was that in the half-century after the 'Great Change', handicraft increasingly replaced mechanization in production, as part of the emergence of social equality, respect for the natural environment of which we are a part, and joy in the creativity of work. Morsom decides to accompany them as far as Oxford. Unexpectedly, Ellen arrives by boat herself to join them, and William joins her in her boat. The two boats proceed beyond Oxford.

28. THE LITTLE RIVER

On the Upper Thames, William tells Ellen that he has in fact himself come from that very 'ugly past' which they have been discussing, but it seems she had already guessed this.

29. A RESTING PLACE ON THE UPPER THAMES

They stop to eat on a beautiful headland, and Ellen asks William to explain further the contradictions of the 'time before Equality of Life', so that it can serve as a warning to avoid the slightest possibility of any future return to such iniquities.

30. THE JOURNEY'S END

Ellen and her father are going to live in Cumberland, and she invites William to go and live there with them. Finally they arrive for their hay-harvesting and are greeted at the river bank by a number of people who have been awaiting their arrival.

31. AN OLD HOUSE AMONGST NEW FOLK

William and Ellen walk to a lovely old house, built before the 'Great Change', which he seems instinctively to know the way to. He wonders what she would have been if she had lived in 'those past days of turmoil and oppression'. In the conversation there are ominous hints of his imminent departure.

32. THE FEAST'S BEGINNING—THE END

Dick takes William for a swim before the great festive dinner which is to take place in a nearby church. On approaching Dick, Clara and Ellen at the dinner table, however, William finds that they do not seem to see him. In despair he walks back towards the house, and is shocked to be greeted on the way by a man in his fifties, curiously familiar looking and quite ragged. Then his vision is dimmed by a great rolling black cloud, and he finds he is back in his bed in dingy Hammersmith, wondering if it was all a dream. He does not despair, however, since 'if others can see it as I have seen it, then it may be called a vision rather than a dream'.

❧ I ❧

The Feast's Beginning:
News from Nowhere and The Utopian Tradition

CHRISTOPHER HAMPTON

> Between us and that which is to be, if art is not to perish utterly,
> there is something alive and devouring; something as it were a
> river of fire that will put all that tries to swim across to a hard
> proof indeed, and scare from the plunge every soul that is not
> made fearless by desire of truth and insight of the happy days
> to come beyond.
>
> Morris: *The Prospects of Architecture*, 1881[1]

IT IS NO ACCIDENT THAT *News from Nowhere*, William Morris's dream-vision of an England transformed by revolutionary action into a socialist commonwealth, should have come to fruition when it did. It was conceived dialectically to register, in the total contrasts it offers, the shock of the historical reality of late-Victorian capitalist society. Projected forward from the gloom and degradation of the age of imperialist expansion Morris was forced to live through, it is the passionate embodiment of a longing for freedom and equality which, rooted in 'the study of history and the love and practice of art', is sharpened by hatred of capitalism and the belief that men and women would one day rise up and sweep aside this noxious system to create a civilization worth living in. As such, and in its challenge to the bankrupt conditions of the time, it is the logical outcome of a lifetime's thought and activity, all that had been implicit in Morris's work from the beginning. And because of the perspectives socialism had opened up to him, Morris was able to grasp the necessary connections between the actual conditions of the life around him and the unrealized possibilities of social experience, and to think ahead toward 'the change beyond the change'[2]—that creation of the grounds for equality of condition without which (in his view) there could be no fulfilment of the potential creative powers of human beings.

This glowing vision of an actualized utopia, 'cast in a form peculiarly suited to the genius of Morris' as 'the crown and climax'[3] of his work, takes its place in the perspectives of history as the culminating achievement of a long and rich tradition, gathering up 'all the riches and experiences of the philosophical Utopias of the intervening period' and relating them 'once again to the neglected hopes of the people'.[4]

Of course, what is common to all the makers of utopia is 'the desire to present their conception of democracy, of social living, of a true commonwealth, in the most popular, most acceptable way'.[5] The Noplace or Nowhere of dream, that is, had to be envisaged, made visible, tangible, attainable. Having its roots in the aspirations and longings of the oppressed, its literary beginnings are to be traced to the songs and poems of those who could not read or write. And among the earliest manifestations of utopian writing, according to Morton,[6] is the early 14th century poem *The Land of Cockaygne,* which describes 'an island of magical abundance, of eternal youth and eternal summer, of joy, fellowship and peace'[7] as an image of hope and desire where class conflicts have been overcome and the poor can at last come into their own. This represents 'the beginning of a dialectical growth of the conception of Utopia';[8] for by the end of the century the struggle against an oppressive system breaks out into active resistance with the Peasants' Revolt, fuelled by the utopian vision of John Ball and Wat Tyler. Indeed, from then on, the dialectic has its reflection at many different levels, and particularly in such documents as the Lollard Petition of 1394, Cade's Manifesto (1450), the poems of Skelton, the anonymous early 16th century *Vox Populi,* the chronicles of Edward Hall, Tyndale's *Parable of the Wicked Mammon* (1528), the Kett Manifesto of 1549, Crowley's work of the mid-16th century, Philip Stubbes' *Anatomy of Abuses* (1583) and the *Annales* of John Stow.[9]

The increasing complexity of the struggle as capitalism took over from the feudal system made it more important to anchor utopia in the minds of its readers or listeners as a place they could recognize and move about in. The more clearly therefore this Nowhere world could be made to resemble the actual world people lived in, however socially transformed, the more likely would it be to convince and encourage as a ground for the struggle to realize the conditions which might bring about fundamental change.

This is one of the most striking features of Sir Thomas More's *Utopia*. Not only is it the first to attempt a fully developed vision of a transformed world; it is firmly anchored in material reality; and as such remains justly the most famous. And in terms of influence—in the scope of its argument, its concept of citizenship and classlessness, of the indispensable part to be played by education in the making of a true commonwealth; and because of its devastating attack upon the money system and the scandalous exploitation of the poor this system condones—it is perhaps the only work of its class that can stand comparison with Morris's. Indeed, Morris himself was well aware of its qualities and excellences, and his view of the book is characteristically generous. He writes:

> We socialists cannot forget these qualities and excellences meet to produce a steady expression of the longing for a society of equality of conditions; a society in which the individual man can scarcely conceive his existence apart from the Commonwealth of which he forms a portion. This, which is the essence of his book, is the essence also of the struggle in which we are engaged. Though doubtless it was the pressure of circumstances in his own days that made More what he was, yet that pressure forced him to give us, not a vision of the triumph of the new-born capitalist society . . . ; but a picture (his own indeed, not ours) of the real New Birth which many men before him had desired, and which now indeed we may well hope is drawing near to realization, though after such a long series of events which at the time of their happening seemed to nullify his own completely'.[10]

He might have said the same for Milton's lifelong battle to maintain the revolutionary aims he had done so much to help bring about. There is the utopian generosity and enthusiasm proclaimed in the 1644 pamphlet *Areopagitica* for the coming harvest of social change;

and his *Defence of the English People*, justifying regicide in the face of Europe. And as defeat for the people and the failure of the revolution loomed close—to end up (as Morris himself puts it) in 'a mongrel condition of things between privilege and bourgeois freedom'[11]—there is his defiant re-affirmation of the struggle in that astonishing work *The Ready and Easy Way to Establish a Free Commonwealth*, where generosity of sentiment, courage and imagination are equally focused upon the prospect and the immediate possibility of creating in England the foundations for a new society grounded upon the civilizing democracy of an educated people. This was published at great personal risk a month before the arrival of Charles II. And by that time of course Milton had already begun *Paradise Lost*, his great negative dialectic of struggle and defeat in which Eden becomes an embodied Utopia, the symbol of a world 'purged and refined, / New Heavens, New Earth, Ages of endless date / Founded in righteousness and peace and love / To bring forth fruits, joy and eternal bliss'.[12]

If Morris saw Milton as among 'the purist Republicans' and acknowledged the Levellers as 'the pioneers of Socialism in that day',[13] he seems to have known nothing about Gerrard Winstanley, though the vision offered in the extraordinary pamphlets produced by the leader of the Diggers between 1648 and 1652 come as close as anyone before Morris to the socio-economic realization of utopian feeling; for Winstanley grounds his concept of the Commonwealth upon the produce of the earth and the social wealth that would follow from its proper distribution.[14]

As for the poets of the Romantic Revolt, the utopian energy and vision generated from and driven by the upheavals of the American and French Revolutions are at their most concentrated in the Prophetic Books of William Blake, which (in Morton's view) 'are utopian from end to end'[15] in their dialectic vision of 'the contrary states of the human soul' and the unending struggle for the 'building up of Jerusalem', the great city of regenerate humanity pitted against the divisive interests of oppressive power.

But Morris seems nowhere to have registered the significance of this work, or indeed that of Wordsworth or Shelley. It is rather the shadow of Keats, as E. P. Thompson puts it—Keats, who 'had found in his poetry a refuge from a social reality which he felt to be unbearably hostile'—that 'falls most markedly upon Morris's youth, and the evidence of his influence may be found in every page of *The Defence of Guenevere*'.[16] As Morris was to comment in 1885: 'We were borne into a dull time oppressed with bourgeoisdom and philistinism so sorely that we were forced to turn back on ourselves, and only in ourselves and the world of art and literature was there any hope'.[17]

At that particular stage of his life, in other words, Morris was in no condition to recognize the significance of Shelley's revolutionary commitment, the kind of utopian defiance that so irradiates his work. What is surprising is that Morris did not later make more of him—particularly in the light of the fact that Shelley, brought up in an England at war, had so unequivocally denounced the callousness and hypocrisy of his class, and considered it the poet's duty to equip himself to resist the tyrannies of his age and to speak for the people, those 'without whom society must cease to subsist'.[18] Of course, Shelley had come too early to be in any position to register the full significance of the industrial transformation being engineered by capitalist organization of the factory system. But he (like Byron) had written passionately about the risings of the working-class, and understood the need for some sort of objective commitment to social change, and for poetry as an active instrument in the struggle for it, which he knew could only be achieved (as he writes in the aftermath of the French Revolution) 'by resolute perseverence and indefatigable hope, and long-suffering and long-believing courage, and the systematic efforts of generations of men of intellect and virtue'.[19]

Morris would surely have responded with delight to Shelley's extraordinary vision of what the future might be should the people rise up and break the power of the 'kings and parasites'[20] who held them down. For indeed in the works of his last three years—poems like *The Mask of Anarchy*, *Prometheus Unbound*, *Hellas*, and *The Triumph of Life*—he makes a sustained attempt to embody the contradictory terms and conditions of a radical utopianism and the disturbing issues it confronted him with, as a cosmic phenomenon centred upon the struggles of humanity. Not that Shelley was free to translate his vision of things into social action; for he had already been effectively marginalized. But he saw his art as an instrument of change ('the trumpet of a prophecy'[21]) and as giving concrete form to the controversial ideas and feelings from which social action springs. For with Shelley, politics and culture, society and the individual, the interests of people and the interests of literature, were aspects of an interactive dialogic process that was everybody's business. What concerned him was not the rhetoric of parties echoing the interests of the few but the clash of ideas and feelings and the sharpening influence of ideas upon the mind and the sensibility. And above all, for him, politics meant raising the level of awareness to a maximum attentiveness, to alert people to the oppressive conditions they were faced with, and to incite them into open conflict with their enemies in the struggle for emancipation. It may be that the inspired utopianism of this quest was often pitched at too high a level. But Shelley knew that inspiration was not enough. The challenge, at a time of singular difficulty for the oppressed, was to put that inspiration to use—to feed it with ideas that would match his instinct, to risk himself and make his words a concentrated voice for the needs of others.

Looking back over the stages of William Morris's development from his affluent middle-class beginnings as a post-Romantic artist nurtured on the negative aesthetics of Keats and the theory and practice of the Pre-Raphaelite movement he became involved in, with its compensatory vision of an alternative world so meticulously rendered in the work of his friends Holman Hunt, Millais, Rossetti and Burne-Jones,[22] one can recognize the first stirring of the fundamental ideas and images which he was to make so much of in the dream-world of *News from Nowhere*. For *News from Nowhere* is shot through with that early enchantment—Hunt's lustrous summery landscapes, Millais' social penetration, the sensuous artifice of Rossetti, and the meticulous attention to detail that went into this very conscious and thoroughgoing attempt to reproduce an ideal past in an age of crass materialism in so many ways the diametric opposite of that imagined world.

What all this early enthusiasm for the beauty of the past lacked was any sort of direct connection with the contradictions, the injustices and the appalling conditions brought into being by the divisive triumphs of industrial capitalism. Indeed, at a certain level

'Pre-Raphaelite versions of Keats or the Bible or Malory were (like the worst of Tennyson's *Idylls*) little more than the projection of the impoverished sensibility of the Victorians into a medieval setting, with conventional Victorian gentlemen and ladies dressed up in fancy costume.' And 'at their best, they were remote and ethereal, saturated with a yearning for values lost to the world, and whose impossibility of realization was accentuated rather than relieved by the materialistic detail of the painting.'[23] The very nature of this imagery, and the drift of Victorian art and culture in post-1848 England is symptomatic of the profound split that had opened up between the new leisured class and the millions of men, women and children whose poverty and exploitation made the wealth on which that leisure was based possible, bringing about the 'terrible spectacle', as Morris was later to put it, 'of two peoples, living street by street, and door by door—people of the same blood, the same tongue, and at least nominally under the same laws—but yet one civilized and the other uncivilized'.[24]

Morris's transformation, in other words, was not sudden. It started from Ruskinian distress and generalized revulsion, and came in stages, step by step, out of the challenge of immediate experience, heralded by the impact of a journey to Iceland, his study of the Norse sagas, the launching of the campaign for the protection of ancient buildings, and his involvement in the controversies over the Eastern Question, which brought him into open collision with the forces of ruling-class prejudice and jingoism. But when it came it brought about a profound and radical change of outlook, which 'broke through the narrowing charmed circle of defeatism of bourgeois culture',[25] and in this sense represents an essential key to any understanding of the imaginative and exploratory nature of Morris's work from the 1880s onward. To read *A Dream of John Ball*, *The Pilgrims of Hope*, *News from Nowhere* and the more directly political writing that forms the groundwork out of which these books were conceived is to register the extraordinary focus of Morris's achievement—his passionate sense of the beauty of the world and its artistic heritage on the one hand, colliding with the impact upon him of the ugliness imposed upon it as a consequence of the capitalist pursuit of profit on the other. But it was his reading of Marx that provided the

connections, set the fuse burning, channelled the energy, and commit-
ted Morris to the utopian perspectives of his vision of the future—
giving him the courage and power, as Thompson points out, to make
that 'leap out of the kingdom of necessity into an imagined kingdom
of freedom in which desire may actually indicate choices or impose
itself as need'.[26]

What sets Morris apart from most of his contemporaries in the
last thirteen years of his life is the insistence of this quest for the fulfilment of utopian desire, matched by his materialist grasp of the study
and practice of history, as generated by 'the tensions of the revolutionary mind'[27] in action towards the transformation of the social order.
Though it had cost him a great deal, his underlying interests—for
long years subterranean and dislocated—were all the time being
strengthened by the anger and frustration, the 'sickness of heart' he
felt, his dreaming sense of the future in the past, his vision of medieval
England. But even as he probed, explored and experimented,
restlessly trying to harness his energies to some kind of meaningful
end, he was to become more and more deeply aware of the ugliness
and squalor of the world he lived in and of what capitalism was doing
to his country and its people. This drove him deeper into himself and
into his art in an anguished search for answers. There were the long
poems beginning with *The Defence of Guinevere* and culminating in
his version of the great Nibelungen Saga, *Sigurd the Volsung*. There
was the painting. There were the meticulous decorative designs he
worked at with such intentness, which were to become the foundation
of his famous business enterprise. There was his passion for architecture and for the lesser arts. In fact, during the 1860s and 70s, 'whatever chanced to be Morris's goal of the moment', as a friend wrote
in 1871, 'was pursued by him with as much intensity as though the
universe contained no other possible goal'.[28] But the pessimism he
felt as he appeared to be moving deeper and deeper into the alienating
trap of his class position—in itself a symptom of his own shocked
sense of frustration—is at its blackest in the poems of *The Earthly
Paradise* of 1869; for as Philip Henderson observes, 'the emotion
underlying Morris's poem is a sense of the emptiness of life'.[29] This
represents almost the lowest point Morris reached along the roman-
ticising path he had started out on, the logical end-product of the

evasive apolitical aesthetics so characteristic of the post- Romantics, leaving him trapped in the imprisoning despair of his class. 'Dreamer of dreams', he writes, 'born out of my due time',

> Why should I strive to set the crooked straight?
> Let it suffice me that my murmuring rhyme
> Beats with light wing against the ivory gate,
> Telling a tale not too importunate
> To those who in the sleepy region stay,
> Lulled by the singer of an empty day.[30]

This Apology to *The Earthly Paradise* catches the melancholy defeatism of mid-19th century poetry. What it demonstrates, here at the nadir of Morris's personal quest for answers, is that the Earthly Paradise is nothing but an illusion and that even the delights the poem registers are mere shadows of reality, insubstantial and tantalising echoes of the living energy of things and of people—in E.P. Thompson's words a 'mechanical oscillation between sensuous luxury and horror, melancholy and despair'.[31]

It is at this bleakest point, nevertheless, that Morris (unlike his friends and mentors) begins to respond to the alienating impact of the social relations determined by the division of labour on both sides of the divide—that process which Marx describes in the *Grundrisse*, as the 'absolute separation between property and labour, between living labour capacity and the conditions of its realization, between objectified and living labour, between value and value-creating activity'.[32] 'What shall I say', Morris was to write of this time in his life, looking back on it from 1894,

> concerning its mastery of and its waste of mechanical power, its commonwealth so poor, its enemies of the commonwealth so rich, its stupendous organization for the misery of life! Its contempt of simple pleasures which everyone could enjoy but for its folly? Its eyeless vulgarity which has destroyed art, the one certain solace of labour? All this I felt then as now, but I did not know why it was so. The hope of the past times was gone, the struggle of mankind for many ages had produced nothing but this sordid, aimless, ugly confusion; the immediate future seemed to me likely to intensify all the present evils by sweeping away the last

survivals of the days before the dull squalor of civilization had settled down on the world. . . . So there I was in for a fine pessimistic end of life, if it had not somehow dawned on me that amidst all this filth . . . the seeds of a great change, what we others call Social-Revolution, were beginning to germinate.[33]

What saved him, gave him strength to break out of the insulated circle of his own class, was his grasp of the perspectives of history, his recognition of the economic material conditions that determined the structure of his world, his intuitive sense of fellowship with the oppressed. To put it in his own words: 'the study of history and the love and practice of art forced me into a hatred of the civilization which, if things were to stop as they are, would turn history into inconsequent nonsense, and make art a collection of the curiosities of the past, which would have no serious relation to the life of the present.'[34].

It was this awareness and his increasing discontent with any sort of detached commentary on the 'rotten sham society'[35] he lived in that took him across the barriers of class and made him a socialist. He had begun to see for himself how deeply the alienating divisiveness of the capitalist system had estranged people from each other, and reduced society to a mere caricature of a real community, since 'all the while its whole energy, its whole organized precision, is employed in one thing, the wrenching of the means of living from others; while outside that everything must be as it may, whoever is the worse or the better for it; as in the war of fire and steel, all other aims must be crushed out before that one object.'[36]

In other words, it was the shock of his reaction to the material conditions determined by a rapacious economic system at work and its devastating consequences for the people of his world that drove him towards commitment and from that to the writing of *News from Nowhere*. He had broken with the bourgeois viewpoint, which in Marx's perception in the *Grundrisse*, had 'never advanced beyond the antithesis between itself and the romantic viewpoint'.[37] He had questioned the system and the extant property values it was nourished on, together with the kind of ideology it generated, which tended either to end up in a mystifying affirmation of human potentiality or to shade off into disillusionment or a consolatory individual happiness—the metaphysical hazard of even the best Victorian novelists: their vision of an amended world coming up against the brutal conditions of material reality, even when these conditions lay just beyond the boundaries of middle-class comfort and could there be dismissed.

It was Morris's thinking about the underlying conditions of his world, and above all his reading of Marx, that set up the necessary interconnections, made him question the central assumptions of his class, brought together the disparate parts he had been so deeply engaged in trying to make sense of, enabled him to break out of the insulating circles within which the terms of cultural (and political) discourse were determined. And the 'crucial confluence' of interests and conditions that confronted him, almost alone among his fellow writers, meant of course that he was faced with the actual presence of the class divide and with the necessity of crossing it, of plunging into what he dauntingly describes as 'a river of fire'—a barrier at once 'alive and devouring' which would 'scare from the plunge' everyone who was not 'made fearless by desire of truth and insight of the happy days to come beyond'.[38]

Once having crossed that river, Morris found himself involved in the business of making socialists, which meant making a different kind of culture. And in taking that difficult step forward, as an artist with a dialectic view of history, for him it could never have been enough to be a realist. Realism on its own, in the world as he knew it, could lead only to despair. One had to look beyond the present, to 'the change beyond the change'. And Morris saw it as his task to create a vision of reality that would take into account the disastrous alienation of men and women from the social and political conditions of their world and the contradictory nature of these conditions. Which is exactly what he set out to do in the writing of the three works culminating with *News from Nowhere*.

The peculiar trance-like quality characteristic of both *A Dream of John Ball* and *News from Nowhere* is given substance and context by Morris's firm grasp of the dialectics of history, in terms of which one period interacts upon another. Out of his own present, the dreamer as protagonist is able to step forward, as someone held in a kind of waking dream, into the imagined world of the past or of the future, precisely as if he were entering that world, making it, defining it as a potentiality. It is tantalizing, it is longed-for, it is *there* as an immediate condition—that which in the past or in the future does not yet exist—at once heightened, caught inside its own atmosphere, and somehow too important to let sink back below the level of consciousness. The dream images, that is, break through the barriers and limitations of the actual present—the squalid conditions of 19th century England—to a world transformed, a world returning to its natural human scale: John Ball's dream of the future as seen through the eyes of the visitant *from* the future; and old Hammond's view of the future-present registered through the eyes of the visitant from the past.

And as Hammond recalls, looking back from the twenty-first century at Morris's own time:

> When the hope of realizing a communal condition of life for all men arose, quite late in the 19th century, the power of the middle classes, the then tyrants of society, was so enormous and crushing, that to almost all men, even those who had, you may say despite themselves, despite their reason and judgement, conceived such hopes, it seemed a dream. So much was this the case that some of those more enlightened men who were then called Socialists, although they well knew, and even stated in public, that the only reasonable condition of Society was that of pure Communism (such as you now see around you), yet shrunk from what seemed to them the barren task of preaching the realization of a happy dream. Looking back now, we can see that the great motive-power of the change was a longing for freedom and equality, akin if you please to the unreasonable passion of the lover; a sickness of heart that rejected with loathing the aimless solitary life of the well-to-do educated men of that time.[39]

A longing for freedom and equality; a sickness of heart—these are the contradictory quickening sources of Morris's socialist aesthetics and of his unequivocal commitment to the cause of the people. Or, to put it another way, it could be said that the starting-point of Morris's vision of reality is his awareness of alienation, his 'sense of the radical dislocation of consciousness from historical reality (with its potential for change)'. And it is from this complex dialectic view of things that he conceives the tasks of art. Art has 'to create a new consciousness that moves away from the immediate towards the possible'. And in order to give art the power to see 'the future in the present ... realism has to be transcended'. Which is not to say that art under capitalism can ever escape the alienating conditions that determine the life of the citizen. What it has to do is to transform these conditions 'into revolutionary consciousness by the recognition of the collective possibilities of the mind's curve away from actuality'. In other words, 'for Morris in dreams begins responsibility'.[40]

It is the insistence of responsibility and of a whole structure of values concerning the place of literature in a world in which the survival of people matters at least as much as the survival of literature that gives such cogency and force to the argument and the form of *News from Nowhere*. Indeed, Morris leaves us in no doubt that people matter more. As Ellen's attack in Chapter xxii upon the social attitudes of certain nineteenth-century novelists makes clear, too many novels (at least in her view) end with 'the hero and heroine living happily in an island of bliss on other people's troubles' after much 'dreary introspective nonsense about their feelings and aspirations, and all the rest of it; while the world must even then have gone on its way, and dug and sewed and baked and built and carpentered round about these useless animals'.[41]

In *News from Nowhere*, through the agency of the dream, Morris is able to look ahead with confidence beyond the disorders of his own world because he is able to perceive, out of the links and perspectives of the past, the stages of a living record that reflects and confirms the continuity of the struggle. 'It is not we', as he says, 'who can build up the new social order; the past ages have done the most of that work for us; but we can clear our eyes to the signs of the times, and we shall then see that the attainment of a good condition of life is being made possible for us, and that it is now our business to stretch out our hands to take it'.[42]

Which is what, in its representation of a world transformed by revolutionary confrontation into 'the New Society of Equality',[43] *News from Nowhere* is all about!

ڪ 2 ڪ

How the Change Came:
News from Nowhere and Revolution

JOHN CRUMP

NEWS FROM NOWHERE derives its reputation more from its wonderfully attractive depiction of communist society than from its account of how communism was achieved. This is not to say that Morris's views on revolution and social change are without value. Far from it. There is much in Morris's description of class struggle and social upheaval that is illuminating and from which we can learn even one hundred years later. Yet it is also true that there are aspects of his account of an imaginary revolution that are unconvincing, contradictory and insufficiently thought out. Hence it is probably fair to say that, if the main purpose of *News from Nowhere* had been to describe a process of revolution and social change, the book would very likely be regarded as a minor work of communism instead of one of the great contributions to communist literature.

The aim of this chapter is to identify the strengths and the weaknesses of Morris's ideas on revolution, as they are revealed in *News from Nowhere*. Before this can be done, however, we need to summarize the description Morris gives of how a communist revolution developed in Britain. Most of what he has to say on the subject comes from the lips of Old Hammond in Chapter XVII of *News from Nowhere*, which is entitled 'How the Change Came'. A summary cannot hope to match the immediacy and excitement conveyed by the original, especially when Old Hammond quotes an eye-witness to a massacre in Trafalgar Square, but a synopsis does provide the opportunity systematically to identify the stages through which Morris saw a communist revolution passing.

Morris's revolution does not emerge from nowhere. It is the outcome of an extended struggle for reforms and the accompanying effort of workers to organize themselves. Various improvements in the position of the workers within capitalism are achieved by these methods, including better conditions of labour, a reduction of working hours, the legal establishment of minimum wage levels and the imposition of price controls on basic necessities. Such reforms are termed by Morris 'steps on the path of "State Socialism"',[1] which was a nineteenth-century expression for what is more commonly known these days as state capitalism. Moves towards state capitalism gather further momentum when the government establishes state enterprises and the upshot of this trend is that 'it tended more and more to upset the commercial system . . . without providing anything really effective in its place'.[2] The result is a succession of economic crises, brought about by the encroachment of 'State Socialism' into capitalist society and the impediments this puts in the way of capital accumulation, culminating in a terrible crisis which, interestingly enough, Morris locates in 1952.

For the workers, economic dislocation means hunger and deprivation, and they react to this by passing the 'Resolution' by a 'solemn and universal vote of the whole of their federated societies'.[3] These 'federated societies' are the labour unions and the 'Resolution' contains the key demand that all natural resources and means of production be transferred into the hands of the 'Combined Workers', as the unions are collectively known. In the eyes of both the workers and the capitalists, the 'Resolution' is regarded as a virtual declaration of class war, leading to stage two of the revolution.

Stage two begins with a mass meeting which is held in Trafalgar Square in the charged atmosphere created by the economic crisis and the 'Resolution'. The meeting is attacked by the police, resulting in five deaths and many more hurt or imprisoned. A further meeting is then organized 'to retort on the authorities'[4] and, although three or four people are again killed, ten or so policemen are crushed to death and the rest chased away, resulting in 'a victory for the people as far as it went'.[5]

At this point, the situation is polarized. Many of the rich flee to the countryside, while those that remain in the cities are enrolled into a militia. Commerce more or less grinds to a halt. The government mobilises its troops but does 'not dare to use them', while the police are over-stretched because 'riots or threats of riots' are everywhere.[6] One development that proves to be of crucial importance is that, although in Manchester several 'popular leaders' are arrested, 'in London a convention of leaders was got together from the Federation of Combined Workmen, and sat under the old revolutionary name of the Committee of Public Safety'.[7] Although, when compared with the government, this Committee of Public Safety initially has few forces at its command, it gradually becomes an alternative source of legitimacy. One of its first acts is to requisition provisions from big stores and to take over several bakeries in order to provide food. Even though it deposits 'papers with the shop managers promising to pay the price' of the goods it has appropriated, the capitalists regard this as a challenge to the very basis of capitalism. 'A deputation of leading commercial people' threatens to take action into its own hands if the government does not arrest the Committee of Public Safety.[8]

Faced with this ultimatum, the government proclaims a state of siege and puts London under martial law. The Committee of Public Safety meanwhile continues with its activities. In addition to arranging food supplies, it does what it can to organize an ill-armed assortment of men and calls another mass meeting in Trafalgar Square. This meeting provides the opportunity for the military to carry out a well-planned massacre. Between 1,000 and 2,000 workers are mown down by machine guns, while a mere six soldiers are killed and a dozen wounded. Nevertheless, it is significant that many of the troops are horrified by their actions and refuse to keep firing into the crowd after the first blood-letting.

The Trafalgar Square massacre takes the revolution into its third stage—that of the general strike. Although initially terrified by the killings, the workers' fear soon gives way to fury at the authorities' actions. This widespread disaffection is reflected in the fact that, when the Committee of Public Safety is arrested and its members brought to trial, the jury acquits them. Having been released from prison, the Committee of Public Safety continues to have a role to play as a symbol of opposition to the government and Parliament. But what is of immensely more importance is the emergence, at grass-roots level, of 'a new network of workmen's associations ... whose avowed single object was the tiding over of the ship of the community into a simple condition of Communism'. It is these 'workmen's associations' (which a twentieth-century writer would probably call 'workers' councils') which become 'the mouthpiece and intermediary of the whole of the working classes'.[9]

In the meantime, the economic crisis has worsened inexorably. A point has been reached where there is 'the rapidly approaching break-down of the whole system founded on the World-Market and its supply'.[10] Alarmed by this prospect, all those who support capitalism tend to close ranks. Guilt-ridden liberals, previously appalled by the army's brutality, bury their consciences and the Liberal government of the day allows itself to be voted out of office by Parliament, to be replaced by an unambiguously pro-capitalist Conservative government. It is this collusion between the capitalist parties which finally destroys any lingering parliamentary illusions entertained by the workers. The 'popular representatives', having attempted 'to fight the matter out by divisions in the House of Commons', walk out of Parliament for good and come over 'in a body to the Committee of Public Safety'.[11]

The next turn of events is that the new Conservative government arrests the Committee of Public Safety and stands poised to unleash its military forces on the revolutionaries. Yet, even though the Committee of Public Safety has by now considerable armed forces of its own, it responds to its own arrest by employing 'a weapon which they thought stronger than street fighting'.[12] This is the general strike, which paralyses the newspapers, communications, the commercial distribution of foodstuffs and so on. Not only is the government confounded by this tactic, since there are no armed revolutionaries against whom it can deploy its soldiers and its police, but it also finds that the arrest of the Committee of Public Safety has not decapitated the revolution. The removal of the Committee of Public Safety has little practical effect, since the centre of gravity of the revolution has already shifted to the workers' councils. The revolution has assumed the form of 'a huge mass of people in thorough sympathy with the movement, bound together by a great number of links of small centres with very simple instructions'.[13] Even more noteworthy is the fact that it is probably this juncture that one can identify with the concrete emergence of communism, albeit in a rudimentary form. No longer is the Committee of Public Safety issuing vouchers as substitute money in payment for requisitioned goods. Rather it is the case that:

> The workmen's committees were extended, and gave relief to great numbers of people, for they had organized a considerable amount of production of food by men whom they could depend upon.[14]

Defeated by the general strike, the government has no option but to release the Committee of Public Safety from prison for the second time and agree to a truce. 'All the definite claims of the people' are conceded and, although many of these demands are trifling and of little more than symbolic value, there is one concession that is of considerable importance:

> This was the claim of recognition and formal status for the Committee of Public Safety, and all the associations which it fostered under its wing. This it is clear meant two things: first, amnesty for 'the rebels', great and small, who, without a distinct act of civil war, could no longer be attacked; and next, a continuance of the organized revolution.[15]

The only concession that is made on the workers' side is that, as a sop to the government and reactionary opinion generally, the Committee of Public Safety renames itself the 'Board of Conciliation and its local offices'.

The fourth and final stage of the revolution is the civil war. In a sense, the successful outcome of the general strike already spells victory for the revolutionary cause. But there are elements among the reactionaries who are not prepared to give up the counter-revolutionary struggle and who are determined to fight on, however hopeless their prospects. Bands of young men from 'the upper and middle classes' organize themselves under the preposterous name of the 'Friends of Order' and engage in guerilla warfare, being joined by officers of the regular army, who 'were mostly the very stupidest men in the country'.[16] Initially, the government pretends to be neutral, but eventually it shows its true colours, joins with the 'Friends of

Order' and the reactionary section of the regular army, and takes on the revolutionary forces.

This turn of events ensures that the revolution must be fought through to nothing less than a communist conclusion, compromise now being impossible:

> The end, it was seen clearly, must be either absolute slavery for all but the privileged, or a system of life founded on equality and Communism.[17]

The civil war lasts about two years and is accompanied by enormous destruction. Awful though this is, Morris implies that it has its positive side. Not only is much that is ugly and harmful within capitalism destroyed, allowing a fresh start to be made on a communist basis, but the struggle has a beneficial effect on the revolutionaries. The needs of the moment draw out from within the working class the organizational skills and other latent talents that the situation demands, causing Old Hammond to reflect that:

> from all I have read and heard, I much doubt whether, without this seemingly dreadful civil war, the due talent for administration would have been developed amongst the working men.[18]

The civil war ends in victory for the working class and the subsequent flowering of communism.

It is now possible to examine various features of the revolution which Morris clearly intends his readers to see as contributing to the successful overthrow of the old order. The first such feature is the class struggle. Although Morris refers in places to the revolutionary 'people' and 'popular' demands, it is the working class that occupies centre stage in the revolutionary drama that he describes. Morris writes as a communist critic of capitalist society and what appals him about this social system is not just that its ugliness and brutality offends his sensitive nature as an artist, but that human community is torn apart by capitalism's class divisions. Yet for Morris the divisive effect of social classes is not a cause merely of dismay and regret. As a communist, he sees not only the negative side of the class struggle but also the promise of human liberation that it contains. In order to represent the negative side of the equation, Morris outlines the view of the working class held by some socialists who, prior to the revolution, are inclined to reformism. These reformists:

> saw the huge mass of the oppressed classes too much burdened with the misery of their lives, and too much overwhelmed by the selfishness of misery, to be able to form a conception of any escape from it except by the ordinary way prescribed by the system of slavery under which they lived; which was nothing more than a remote chance of climbing out of the oppressed into the oppressing class.[19]

Morris is generous to a fault when he writes that the strategy pursued by the reformists was, theoretically at any rate, 'not altogether unreasonable', but equally he reveals that his own assessment of the working class's potential is fundamentally different from that of the reformists when he refers to the 'instinct for freedom' of this 'slave-class'. Even if most wage slaves had no clear picture of 'the happiness of a free life' and 'could not look forward to the happiness or peace' of the new society, they did 'at least look forward to the war which a vague hope told them would bring that peace about'.[20]

The importance of the class struggle is also underlined by the various stages through which the revolution passes. The crucial breakthrough in the revolution is not achieved by the undifferentiated 'people' flocking to the barricades, but by the wage workers using the power which derives from their role as the producers of wealth within capitalism. By refusing any longer to produce profits for the bosses, they force the capitalist government to accede to their demands. Looked at from the other side of the class divide, the civil war breaks out because, even though from a rational point of view it may be obvious that the days of capitalism are numbered, members of the aristocracy and the capitalist class find the impending loss of their property and privileges such a painful prospect that they lash out in illogical rage. Hence, for Morris, the class struggle is both the ultimate source of the revolution and influences the course it takes at each stage of its development.

A second feature of Morris's revolution, which is not unconnected with the first, is the importance attributed to working class self-liberation, and the accompanying playing down of the role of leadership. Revolution is portrayed by Morris as a process whereby workers learn to organize themselves and develop the ability to administer their own affairs in their own collective interest. Leaders are not entirely absent from this process, but their role is largely symbolic. Prominent individuals, like the members of the Committee of Public Safety, might be useful as symbols of revolt and galvanizers of resistance, but they do not lead the revolution. No individuals are irreplaceable in the revolutionary struggle and no party orchestrates the action. In contrast to capitalist revolutions, which elevate certain 'great men' as they unfold (and hence are pregnant with a new ruling class), the role played by the Committee of Public Safety diminishes as the communist revolution progresses.

It has already been noted that the centre of gravity of the revolution progressively shifts to Morris's 'workmen's associations' and that a twentieth-century author would probably have used the term 'workers' councils' to describe these organizations of working class self-administration. What is remarkable about Morris's account written in 1890, is that easily recognizable in his description of grass-roots bodies which are thrown up spontaneously in the heat of revolutionary struggle are the workers' councils that emerged historically for the first time only fifteen years later in the Russian revolution of 1905. In Morris's revolution it is these workmen's associations/workers' councils which both guarantee that the revolutionary movement will be multifocal (and hence will not be dominated by a centralized leadership) and provide an environment in which workers' initiative can flourish. Far from being in a position to lead the revolution, the old members of the Committee of Public Safety 'had little administrative capacity', thus leaving the ground clear for organizational links and an administrative structure to crystallize among the broad mass of revolutionary workers.[21] This trend is enhanced as the revolution gathers momentum and reaches its climax in the general strike and the civil war. Morris's vision of a process of working class self-liberation that is largely free from leadership stems from the strategy encapsulated in the maxim of the International Working Men's Association that 'the emancipation of the working class must be the act of the working class itself'.[22]

A third feature of Morris's account of a communist revolution is the vital importance of understanding, and the part played by socialist education in bringing this about. Although the heroes of Morris's revolution are the ordinary workers in their rank and file organizations, he is far from glamourizing the working class. Morris was too aware of the brutalizing effect of capitalism to pretend that there was anything noble about wage labourers. Capitalism reduces a 'vast number of working people' to a condition in which they are 'used to act as their masters drove them, or rather as the system drove, of which their masters were a part'.[23] Workers who are in the habit of taking orders from their bosses are not the raw material from which a new society can be constructed. Even if the old system collapses and the pressures that have previously acted on workers with this attitude are removed, they will not respond by behaving as free, co-operative human beings. Rather, without any other influences acting on them, Morris expects that 'nothing but the mere animal necessities and passions of men would have any hold on them'.[24] In the revolution that Morris describes, one factor that prevents the generalization of such self-centred and destructive attitudes, which would produce nothing more than mere social breakdown, is the educational effect of socialist propaganda. The mass of the working class 'had been leavened by Socialist opinion in the first place, and in the second place by actual contact with declared Socialists, many or indeed most of whom were members of those bodies of workmen'.[25] Morris believes that it is to this end that socialists have a key role to play in spreading socialist ideas among their fellow workers.

However, Morris was too much of a materialist to imagine that the force of ideas alone, even socialist ideas, could somehow retrieve a situation that otherwise teetered on the brink of imminent social breakdown. In his eyes, socialist education is not reducible to a set of ideas that is acquired by the working class solely thanks to the efforts of socialists. Morris took the view that understanding of communism is acquired, at least in part, through the workers' own activity in a communist revolution. For Morris, communist revolution is not simply a process whereby the working class changes the purpose and organization of society. Part and parcel of a communist revolution is that, in struggling to change society, workers also change themselves. In line with this perception of the educational effect of revolutionary struggle, Morris does not suggest that communist revolution comes on to the agenda only when a sufficient number of workers have had their otherwise empty heads filled with socialist propaganda. Rather it is that, through their own experiences of struggle, first within capitalism and ultimately against capitalism, workers come to understand not only how to fight but also what it is they are fighting for. In the first stage of a communist revolution workers might be conscious of little more than the facts that they are oppressed and that they do not need the bosses, although the bosses need them.[26] As successive stages of the revolution are experienced, so workers' organizational skills and grasp of the situation are enhanced, until a point is reached where:

> I will not say that the people of that time foresaw the life we are leading now, but there was a general instinct amongst them towards the essential part of that life, and many men saw clearly beyond the desperate struggle of the day into the peace which it was to bring about.[27]

Morris impresses on his readers that communist revolution does not depend on inspired leaders, but consists of masses of ordinary workers deepening their understanding of communism as they advance further along the revolutionary path, all the while benefiting from the educational activities of the socialists within their own ranks.

The final feature of Morris's account of a communist revolution to which attention needs to be drawn is the contempt in which he holds Parliament. It speaks volumes that, having described the workers' councils as 'the mouthpiece and intermediary of the whole of the working classes', he continues:

> and the manufacturing profit-grinders now found themselves powerless before this combination; unless *their* committee, Parliament, plucked up courage to begin the civil war again, and to shoot right and left, they were bound to yield to the demands of the men whom they employed, and pay higher and higher wages for shorter and shorter day's work.[28]

Parliament figures in *News from Nowhere* as an instrument of the capitalists and a setting for double-dealing, so that its only point of contact with the revolution is when the 'popular representatives' withdraw from the House of Commons and come over to the Committee of Public Safety. Parliament is presented as irrelevant to the working class, and the communist revolution is depicted as an extra-parliamentary struggle, fought out on the streets and at the point of production (in the general strike).

The only people for whom Morris's handling of this issue is likely to pose problems are those who equate democracy with parliamentary institutions. What Morris is pointing out to his readers is that Parliament does not even remotely approximate to an organ of genuine democracy. Old Hammond asks the rhetorical question:

> Was not the Parliament on the one side a kind of watch-committee sitting to see that the interests of the Upper Classes took no hurt; and on the other side a sort of blind to delude the people into supposing that they had some share in the management of their own affairs?[29]

Morris believes that this is indeed the case and that, in contrast to Parliament, it is the communist revolution which is really democratic. The communist revolution is democratic because, in the first place, it pits the oppressed majority against those who are seeking to defend minority privileges. Secondly, and more important however, the communist revolution is democratic not simply because it is in the interests of a majority but because, through the organizations they have constructed, the working class majority can, in a direct and unmediated fashion, shape their own destiny and control their own lives. Morris tells us frustratingly little about the workers' councils but, from the limited sketch he does provide, their essential features can be discerned. Clearly they are mass, grass-roots organizations. As 'mouthpieces', they directly express the views of their members, rather than, in the style of Parliament, taking decisions on behalf of constituents who have forfeited all rights once elections have taken place. And, as 'intermediaries', they are horizontally arranged bodies for communicating and negotiating, rather than vertically aligned structures with ruling and controlling functions, again as typified by parliamentary government.

Morris's view of a communist revolution occurring beyond and against Parliament is at one with the other features of the imaginary revolution that we have been considering. Morris's revolution is anti-parliamentary precisely because it is based on the class struggle, precisely because it is an act of workers' self-liberation that dispenses with leadership and precisely because it is informed by an understanding of communism.

One problem raised by Morris's account of 'how the change came' is that he limits his description to the confines of a single nation-state. Too much should not be made of this. Certainly, it would be unfair to suggest that Morris imagined that communism could be achieved within a single country, be it Britain or any other. The realized communist society takes in a good part, if not all, of the world, for as Old Hammond puts it in Chapter XIV:

> I will tell you at once that the whole system of rival and contending nations which played so great a part in the 'government' of the world of civilization has disappeared along with the inequality betwixt man and man in society.[30]

Be that as it may, Morris's account of a communist revolution is confined solely to events in Britain and this is unfortunate. The reasons for this could well have been literary rather than ideological, in that Morris might have shrunk from the difficult task of attempting to portray the revolution on an international rather than a national scale. All the same, there were devices he could have used to circumvent this difficulty. Even on a national scale, his account of the communist revolution is largely confined to London. Provincial centres such as Manchester and Glasgow are given only brief mentions, merely to indicate that the revolution is proceeding in the provinces as well as in the capital. It would not have stretched Morris's literary skills much further to have included similar passing references to, for example, Paris and Berlin.

Whatever the reason for this oversight, it is regrettable because it might be taken as implying that, by means of a successful communist revolution, a single country could withdraw from the worldwide system of production for profit. Not only is this impossible under circumstances where the capitalist world market dominates the decisions taken about production in every corner of the globe, but equally the momentous events which Morris describes as taking place in Britain could not have occurred without causing major repercussions in other countries. By the time Morris was writing in the late nineteenth century, capital was an international phenomenon and the extent of trans-national investment was already considerable. Similarly, the working class was already open to international influences, as evidenced by the spread of social-democratic illusions from one country to another during the years of Morris's political activity. Hence it is inconceivable that class warfare on the scale that Morris relates could have been fought out in Britain without provoking class conflict and influencing events elsewhere.

A second weakness in Morris's account of a communist revolution, and probably a more serious one, is the attitude he takes towards 'State Socialism'. The role Morris allots to 'State Socialism' during the build up to full-scale communist revolution is that of an agency which undermines capitalism and puts the capitalist class on the defensive. Presented in this fashion, 'State Socialism' could be interpreted by readers of *News from Nowhere* as an anti-capitalist form which, objectively at any rate, works in communism's favour in the struggle against capitalism. Yet, if we examine the concrete policies which Morris details as comprising 'State Socialism', we find that, without exception, they consist of reforms implemented *within* the framework of existing capitalist society. These reforms (improved conditions of labour, reduction in working hours, minimum wage levels etc.) impose certain regulations on the relationship between capital and wage labour, but in no way do they abolish that relationship, which stands at the very heart of capitalism. Even the state enterprises that are established under the auspices of 'State Socialism' are evidently still engaged in commodity production since, when the economic crisis of 1952 occurs, they are at least as severely affected as private companies:

> the partial inefficient government factories, which were terribly jobbed, all but broke down and a vast part of the population had for the time being to be fed on undisguised 'charity' as it was called.[31]

Thus everything we are told about 'State Socialism' leads inevitably to the conclusion that, far from representing an assault on capital, it is nothing more than a modified version of capitalism itself. It is in recognition of the real nature of 'State Socialism' that, in subsequent years, it has come to be known as state *capitalism*. Unfortunately, however, Morris reveals in *News from Nowhere* that he is far from having grasped that 'State Socialism' is an unalloyed form of capitalism. The 'establishment of government factories for the production of necessary wares, and markets for their sale' is described by him as 'a measure hostile to the masters', while 'the spread of communistic theories, and the partial practice of State Socialism had at first disturbed, and at last almost paralysed the marvellous system of commerce under which the old world had lived so feverishly'.[32] In line with Morris's confusion about the nature of 'State Socialism', he harboured illusions about the effect of reforms on the standing of the capitalist class. Referring to the capitalists at the time when the 'Combined Workers' pass the 'Resolution', he writes as follows:

> as they were in many ways still very powerful, or seemed so to be, they still hoped by means of brute force to regain some of what they had lost, and perhaps in the end the whole of it.[33]

Such remarks beg the question: what had the capitalists supposedly 'lost' as a result of a series of piecemeal, state capitalist reforms? Surely it was the very fact that their ownership of capital was still intact that made a revolution necessary. Had state capitalist reforms really been eroding their position, the evolutionary process could have been allowed to take its course and revolution avoided. Morris failed to realize this and consequently quite misread the impact of state capitalist measures on the capitalists' grip on the means of life. In this way, the clear boundary between state capitalism and communism was blurred and the illusion was fostered that these incompatible social formations had elements in common.

To turn to a third weakness in Morris's account, we have already seen that, as the communist revolution progresses, it is the workers' councils which increasingly provide an organizational structure within which working class initiative and action can take place, while the Committee of Public Safety acquires a mainly symbolic importance. Nevertheless, the Committee of Public Safety undoubtedly functions as a rallying point for resistance to capitalism at various crucial stages of the revolution and there is never any doubt expressed about its commitment to the revolutionary struggle. Bearing in mind that the Committee of Public Safety derives from the leadership of the Federation of Combined Workmen (in other words, the union movement), this raises the question of Morris's attitude towards the labour unions and their leaders.

In general, Morris takes an extremely rosy view of the union leaders. Old Hammond recollects that those who formed themselves into the Committee of Public Safety were mostly 'honest, courageous men', which certainly characterizes *News from Nowhere* as a fictional work, in view of the behaviour of most real-life union bureaucrats over the past hundred years. It is true that not all leaders of the Federation of Combined Workmen are presented as paragons of virtue. Despite the passage of time, Old Hammond is still physically discomforted when he recalls the careerism of some union leaders. Yet, conveniently (one might say over-conveniently) the deepening economic and social crisis eliminates such opportunists. Things reach such a pitch that they are 'too dangerous for mere traitors and self-seekers, and one by one they were thrust out and mostly joined the declared reactionaries'.[34] Other fortuitous circumstances also conspire to propel the union leaders/Committee of Public Safety ever forward along the path that leads them away from the role of reformist bureaucrats to that of symbols of revolutionary struggle. To take just one example, we find that when confronted with martial law on the eve of the great massacre in Trafalgar Square,

> the Committee of Public Safety, whatever they thought of their position . . . had now gone too far to draw back; and many of them, it seems, thought that the Government would not act.[35]

While it may be impossible to dismiss such a turn of events out of hand, a severe strain may nevertheless be imposed on the credulity of many of Morris's readers. We know that the unions comprising the Federation of Combined Workmen are long-standing organizations which are equipped with leaders and substantial accumulated reserves ('a biggish fund of money for the support of strikes').[36] We are asked to believe that the leaders of these unions are prepared to risk everything, including their positions, their organizations and the funds at their disposal, in pursuit of a general strike and a rapidly escalating confrontation with a ruling class which will stop at nothing to defend its privileges. Moreover, even when isolated in prison, they unanimously reject the blandishments of the authorities and stand firm for the revolution. Maybe it really did happen just as Morris tells it but, if so, the workers in his novel are lucky indeed to be led by a different breed of men from the union bureaucrats most of us have observed going about their business in the real world.

Morris's handling of the labour unions is a specific example of a general criticism that can be levelled at his account of a communist revolution. In general he employs a 'best scenario' technique to take the revolution on from one stage to the next. Morris seems to have found it difficult to envisage the degree of brutality that the ruling class would employ as it fought to preserve its rule. At the height of the general strike, it is a strangely civilized form of repression that he describes. The 'offices of the Federated Workmen' and the works where the 'Socialist papers' are printed are not attacked,[37] and the government refrains from treating 'their army as a real army, and [using] them strategically as a general would have done, looking on the people as a mere open enemy to be shot at and dispersed wherever they turned up'.[38] In the real world of capitalist viciousness, events rarely turn out so advantageously for the working class. This is one reason why, in a real communist revolution, workers would be well advised to abandon the bureaucratized structure of the unions at an early opportunity and rely on organizations under their direct control, such as the workers' councils.

Throughout the writing of this chapter, it has played on my mind how incongruous it is that, one hundred years after the event, we should be considering the strengths and weaknesses of Morris's account of a revolution located nowhere except in his imagination, instead of assessing the outcome of a struggle for communism enacted here in the real world. The fact is that Morris wrote about a communist revolution that is still unrealized and about a new society that remains a dream. Why, then, did Morris devote his talents to a revolutionary cause whose prospects were far from certain? The question is probably as pointless as asking why Morris expended his energy on artistic works. An artist transmits a landscape to canvas for no better reason than that it is there in all its charm and beauty, and Morris struggled against capitalism for no better reason than that it existed in all its ugliness and brutality. The century that has elapsed has provided no example of a revolution that even remotely approximates to the one Morris described [except perhaps that in Spain in 1936—*editor*]. Capitalism remains impregnable . . . and yet one hundred years later, there is still the same relative handful as in Morris's day to dream the dream and continue the struggle. We communist dreamers have not succeeded in removing the blight of capitalism from the world, but neither has capitalism succeeded in eradicating the dream of communism. The final scene of the drama has yet to be enacted and only then will we know whether Morris's account of a communist revolution is a dream of Nowhere or a dream of Everywhere. At this stage of the action, only one thing is certain: the more dreamers there are, the less it becomes a dream.

ക 3 ക

How Matters Are Managed:
Human Nature and Nowhere

STEPHEN COLEMAN

THE INHABITANTS OF NOWHERE are eminently pleasant folk. In our own age, which is haunted by relentless anxieties about predatory muggers on the streets and mad militarists with their peace-securing bombs, we are not accustomed to expecting from human beings the simple, co-operative decency of Nowhere's people. We are conditioned to be discomforted by such a vision of human pleasantness. In our society, when a stranger smiles at us we assume that he is either an insurance salesman or a politician: in either case the policies on offer will probably do us no good and we would be wise not to smile back. Offered goods or services without payment, we suspect that there will be a catch. Seeing a community of friends co-operating joyously, we become cynically suspicious, presuming that either they are on drugs or there is a guru in the background manipulating their joy. In our society the thoroughly happy person, contented with both life and work, is regarded more often than not as a simpleton; the peaceful human being who seeks to be at one with nature is ridiculed as a social freak, eccentrically oblivious to the 'fact' that life is a jungle and humans are far from pleasant beasts.

Given such low conventional expectations about what human behaviour is like, it is of little wonder that some readers have regarded with incredulity the people described in *News from Nowhere*. Students, asked to comment on Morris's vision, will often praise it as an appealing utopia, but dismiss its characters as being incompatible with conceivable reality. Behaviour which is incongruent with existing social conventionality is defined as utopian. The critics of utopian thought dismiss visions of transformed human behavioural

75

relationships as being intrinsically unrealistic: contrary to human nature. Out of such reasoning emerges a profoundly conservative conclusion about the fixed nature of human behaviour and the relative immutability of social relations.

The behaviour of the people of Nowhere conflicts radically with the image of the human jungle. The Guest, arriving in Nowhere as an escapee from the civilized indecency of Victorian London, observes that 'most people seem thoroughly happy'.[1] In the Guest House in Hammersmith the people exhibit 'unanxious happiness and good temper'.[2] The citizens encountered at Hampton Court 'had an indefinable kind of look of being at home and at ease . . .'[3] The haymakers, working hard in the fields, display 'the height of good temper and enjoyment'.[4] The children seen are 'fine specimens of their race' and are 'clearly enjoying themselves to the utmost'.[5] In the market (where goods are no longer sold, property having been abolished) there are several 'thoughtful' faces which are characterized by 'great nobility of expression', and as for the rest, 'none . . . had a glimmer of unhappiness, and the greater part . . . were frankly and openly joyous'.[6] After some initial doubts about Dick's sanity, the Guest observes the 'peculiarly pleasant and friendly look about his eyes'.[7] Clara also admires Dick's 'good-natured face'.[8] Ellen, whose virtually flawless humanity infatuates the Guest, impresses him most because all that she said and did 'was all done in a new way, and always with that indefinable interest and pleasure of life . . .'[9] This intense and ever-visible love of life—Morris was to call it the Religion of Humanity—pervades all of this new society 'peopled now with this lovely folk, who had cast away riches and attained to wealth'.[10]

Lest the reader be left in any doubt that Nowhere is anything less than a society abundant in human happiness, Old Hammond's words clarify the position and sharpen the contrast between Nowhere and the age we are still in:

> . . . the men and women who go to make up humanity are free, happy and energetic, at least, and most commonly beautiful of body also, and surrounded by beautiful things of their own fashioning, and a nature bettered and not worsened by contact with mankind.[11]

For such people it is 'a point of honour . . . not to be self-centred'.[12] Thought of bliss beyond the grave (the religious 'sigh of the oppressed' which had served a purpose in a society which had deprived the multitude of earthly comfort) is pointless, for 'we are too happy, both individually and collectively, to trouble ourselves about what is to come hereafter.'[13] Freed from worries of poverty and exploitation, suppression of liberty and cultural degradation, who could easily dismiss Hammond's promise that 'the more you see of us, the clearer it will be to you that we are happy'?[14]

Who would dismiss such promise? Most writers in the Judeo-Christian tradition for a start.[15] This tradition is rooted in a theory of innate, limited human nature, rejection of which constitutes a utopian heresy. This is not to say that all utopian writers have rejected the Judeo-Christian conception of human nature (More did not question inherent sinfulness, but sought to regulate and regiment human lives so that people would have to behave harmoniously), but a key element in the definition of utopian visions is their claim to transcend the fixed limits of what non-utopians call human nature. If the utopians are right, and human behaviour is endlessly mutable and dynamic, then *News from Nowhere* can be seen as more than a fantasy of how humans should live ideally, and fulfils Morris's intention of being a vision of how humans could live, materially. Central to the plausibility of Morris's vision, then, is the question of how far humans can go in re-fashioning our social behaviour. What, if any, are the limits of human nature?

If Utopian 'Man' is essentially content in his oneness with nature, Judeo-Christian 'Man' is fundamentally miserable in his innate estrangement from the Platonic One, or God. For the Judeo-Christians, post-Adamic human nature is rooted in sin; the flawed nature of humans is the result of their fallen condition. Sin is that inborn state of human disjunction from God's immaculate perfection. As sinners, humans must abandon all hope of self-perfectibility: the most that can be sought after is God's grace and forgiveness, redeeming humans from the most miserable of fates, but never eliminating the legacy of sin which all generations must inherit in the form of a metaphysical human disease. This is an extremely miserable idea of human nature, antithetical to the boundless hopes of the utopians.

Writing of this so-called original sin, St Augustine, the most influential thinker in the formation of the Christian conception of human nature, states that 'God, the Author of all natures, but not of their defects, created man good, but man, corrupt by choice and condemned by justice, has produced a progeny that is both corrupt and condemned.' From this 'depraved source' humans find themselves faced with a living 'death which has no end, from which they alone are exempt who are freed by the grace of God'.[16] The pessimistic shadow of Augustinian ideology dominated the thinking of medieval society, stifling vision and repressing political hopes of human self-improvement. Some of the Renaissance Catholics, such as Pico della Mirandola, began to contemplate ideas of humans aspiring to godlike self-perfection, but the rise of Protestantism disposed of such heresies, driving human nature even further into the fixed mould of original sin. Martin Luther, the father of Protestantism, was inspired by the writings of Augustine, especially those devoted to repudiating the heresy of Pelagius who had contended that humans could perfect themselves. Luther concluded that humans must abandon all thought of self-reliance and seek whatever happiness they might achieve through Divine Grace. Calvin well summed up this protestant position: 'our will is not only destitute and idle of good, but so fruitful and fertile of sin that it cannot be idle'. Indeed, 'there is more worth in all the vermin of the world than there is in Man, for he is a creature in whom the image of God has been effaced.'[17] One could not imagine a Calvinist writing *News from Nowhere*, less still finding Nowhere's inhabitants human.

When most non-utopian thinkers conceive of humanity it is Fallen Man of whom they think. Thomas Hobbes, defending the need for the fear-inducing State (which has, of course, been dispensed with in Nowhere) asserts that 'Men from their very birth, and *naturally*, scramble for everything they covet, and would have all the world, if they could, to fear and obey them.'[18] Such a belief in the need for the natural inclinations of humans to be controlled and repressed proceeds from Hobbes, the statist, to Edmund Burke, the great theoretician of conservative ideology. Burke regarded it as imperative that 'the passions of individuals should be subjected' and 'the inclinations of men should frequently be thwarted . . . by a power out of themselves; and not, in the exercise of its function, subject to that will and to those passions which it is in office to bridle and subdue.' In short, humans require a power beyond our control to protect us against the deep-seated passions which fester within our natures. This anti-utopian ideology has survived into our own times, either in its unadulterated form of man as a sinner, or else supported by corrupted versions of Darwinist (Man the Predator) or Freudian (Man the Egotist) dystopian prejudices. Whatever its form, the substantial content of the ideology remains intact: the human being is an essentially uncooperative, indecent animal. So, not only can it be stated by a modern Tory philosopher that private property is an 'absolute and ineradicable need' which is instinctively 'rooted in human nature',[19] but it can be stated in a respected liberal newspaper by a respected writer of children's fiction that 'the human is not a very nice animal' and is best described by the terms 'greedy, cruel, foul'.[20] And, while one reputable columnist for a Sunday newspaper informed her readers that 'The desire to have and to hold, to screech at the neighbours and say "Mine all mine" is in our nature . . . ',[21] *The Sunday Times* in a Murdochian tirade against 'communism', asserts that 'You have only to watch two toddlers squabbling over a toy—in Moscow, London or Bombay—to understand that individual property is a basic human desire. The only way to remove it is to beat it out.'[22] Such random illustrations are indicative of the pervasiveness of this ideology—Human Racism is how we might describe it—which inclines its believers to be deeply suspicious of the potentiality for widespread human co-operation and contentment.

Despite the intellectual hegemony of the Augustinian doctrine, the image of sinless humans was not wholly eliminated. Pelagius, a British lay monk of the fifth century, was condemned as a heretic for refusing to accept the notion of original sin. The Pelagian heresy was probably the most subversive threat to Christian human-nature theory to have ever been raised within the faith: if, as Pelagius and his followers argued, sin is not inherent but is a habit which can be defeated by will rather than divine grace, then the project of human self-improvement, indeed self-perfection, is no longer unthinkable. With the Pelagian heresy the prospect of utopia forced its way on to the agenda of social action. While the Pelagians were endeavouring to relieve *Homo sapiens* of the burden of sin, other Christian visionaries sought to revive the sinless imagery of the Garden of Eden by embarking upon literary excursions into pre-Fall Golden Ages. Their writings constituted a richly utopian medieval literature. For example, St Brendan, an Irish monk of the sixth century, describes, in a contemporarily popular Latin legend, his discovery of the Earthly Paradise where 'The clouds never gathered . . . to shade the brightness of the sun. The inhabitants of this place will never suffer from heat, cold, sadness, hunger, thirst, poverty, nor other adversity. They will have a supply of all good things . . .'[23] By the thirteenth century another detailed account of the Golden Age rediscovered was enjoying widespread popularity: the *Tractatus de Purgatorio Sancti Patricii (The purgatory of St Patrick)*. The visitor reports seeing 'a number of people of both sexes as he thought no one had ever seen in this life or he believed the rest of the world to contain . . .' These strange utopian humans 'walked about joyfully' and 'took pleasure in one another's company'.[24] Two elements combine in these early utopian accounts: firstly, pure physical fantasies, such as visions of permanent sunshine and the absence of heat or coldness; such fantasizing reaches a delightful literary peak in the fourteenth-century folk poem, *The Land of Cockaygne,* where the geese fly around ready-roasted and asking to be eaten. The second element in these utopian visions is the depiction of transformed human behaviour. Here are humans, but they are pleasant, gentle, joyous folk, living naturally, yet unafflicted by what orthodox Christianity had defined as human nature.

The Christians were right to declare Pelagian thought heretical, for if humans are capable of perfecting themselves, who needs God's grace? It was not a huge leap—though it took twelve centuries to take—from the Pelagian heresy and the emergence of a utopian theory of behaviour to Locke's claim that the human character is largely the product of upbringing. Following this Lockean perception, the thinkers of the Enlightenment celebrated the plasticity of human behaviour. Liberated from the stultifying belief that they were born sinners, why should human fellowship be dismissed any longer as a utopian proposition?

Utopian socialists before Morris, such as Robert Owen and Charles Fourier, saw no obstacle to the success of co-operative communities once humans were educated to the task of living in them. Morris did not share their confidence. He did not dispute the optimism of the early socialists regarding the potential for human co-operation, but, as a Marxist, Morris could only anticipate successful co-operation within certain material circumstances. Arguing that the capitalist 'system of Society is based on a state of perpetual war', Morris claimed that the motivation towards competitive behaviour could not be overcome simply by an act of ethical will.[25] The system engendered conflict, but Morris pointed out a crucial 'difference between the position of the workers and the profit-makers; to the latter, the profit-grinders, war is necessary; you cannot have profit-making without competition, individual, corporate and national; but you may work for a livelihood without competing; you may combine instead of competing.'[26] In short, conflict is endemic to working-class life under capitalism, but co-operation is stimulated within the same class of people in their struggles to resist the system.

The prerequisite for human fellowship, as far as Morris was concerned, is the establishment of a classless society. This did not mean that all people had to become the same. Not only did Morris reject such a prospect as being culturally diminishing, but his thinking about human nature was sufficiently sophisticated for him to understand that the absence of human inequality did not require a mechanistic and unrealizable eradication of natural human differences. Morris made explicit this recognition in a lecture delivered in 1888 entitled *What Socialists Want*:

> Socialists no more than other people believe that persons are naturally equal: there are amongst men all varieties of disposition, and desires, and degrees of capacity; nevertheless these differences and inequalities are very much increased by the circumstances amongst which a man lives and by those that surrounded the lives of his parents: and these circumstances are more or less under the control of society . . . So you see whatever inequality I admit among people, I claim this equality that everybody should have full enough food, clothes, and housing, and full enough leisure, pleasure and education; and that everybody should have a certainty of these necessaries: in this case we should be equal as Socialists use the word . . .[27]

Morris's conception of human nature was essentially Marxist: a distinction was drawn between biological nature and historical behaviour; the culture of men and women was seen as being principally, though not exclusively, determined by the economic relationships they find themselves in; alienation was regarded not as a metaphysical estrangement between Man and God, but between creative, conscious humans and their broadest productive (including artistic) powers. Morris rejected entirely all religious and metaphysical beliefs about the nature of human beings. Although he had been sent to Oxford University where his mother hoped that he would train for the clergy, Morris tired of theology and dismissed religion. Once, after speaking at the Leicester Secular Society, Morris was advised by a clergyman that socialism was 'an impossible dream' that 'would need God Almighty himself to manage it'. Morris responded, 'Well, damn it man, you catch your God Almighty—we'll have him!'[28]

In *News from Nowhere* Morris repudiates the idea of naturally limited human behaviour. Speaking of the upbringing of people under capitalism, Hammond offers a materialist account of human *nurture*. Of the education of children in the age of Gradgrind, Hammond speaks of how, once 'thrust into schools', children were given

> a niggardly dole of not very accurate information; something to be swallowed by the beginner in the art of living whether he liked it or not, and was hungry for it or not; and which had been chewed and digested over and over again by people who didn't care about it.

Such forced fact-feeding ignored 'the fact of *growth*, bodily and mental'.[29] If capitalist schooling stunted mental growth, the squalid slum dwellings which were made available to the poor are described as 'stews for rearing and breeding men and women in such degradation that that torture should seem to them mere ordinary and natural life'.[30] This was the point: the process of capitalist nurture conditioned humans to see as natural conditions and relationships which were in reality historical, relative and transient. So it is that the citizen of Nowhere, Henry Morsom, bewildered by the past age's dismissal of the 'aspiration after complete equality which we now recognize as the bond of all happy human society', comments that 'This opinion

... seemed as natural then as it seems absurd now ...'[31] When the Guest first encounters Dick he has to confess that 'I began to be afraid that the man was mad, though he looked sane enough.'[32] Indeed, a boatman offering his services freely to passing strangers may well be advised to seek pyschiatric help in our present money-mad society, but it is only the economic conditioning which accompanies the system of wage labour and capital which generates the feeling that paid labour is 'sane' and free service is 'mad'. Amongst the Panare of Venezuela, where an exchange economy does not prevail, it is considered the worst kind of insult to offer a person a wage for a service. A Panare encountering Dick the boatman would entertain no natural doubt about the sanity of this kindly being.

Whereas under capitalism humans were conditioned to behave in economically necessary anti-social ways, in Nowhere the cultivation of co-operative behaviour is not imposed, but reflects the spontaneous harmony between the people and their environment. Hammond explains:

> We have been living for a hundred and fifty years, at least, more or less in our present manner, and a tradition or habit of life has been growing on us; and that habit has become a habit of acting on the whole for the best. It is easy for us to live without robbing each other. It would be possible for us to contend with and rob each other, but it would be harder for us than refraining from strife and robbery. That is in short the foundation of our life and our happiness.[33]

Having a common social interest, instead of the class antagonisms of times past, a process of cultural regeneration has been stimulated in Nowhere's people. This sounds fine, but the poor record of utopian thinkers when it comes to cultivating habits of behaviour in their regenerated citizens must be acknowledged if we are to see whether Morris has done any better. Utopian character-building has been a predominantly authoritarian tradition. In More's *Utopia* harmony is achieved at the expense of the most severe social regimentation and indoctrination. The young are 'educated' by priests who train them to conform to the utopian arrangements of life:

They do their utmost to ensure that, while children are still at an impressionable age, they're given the right ideas about things—the sort of ideas best calculated to preserve the structure of their society. If thoroughly absorbed in childhood, these ideas will persist throughout adult life, and so contribute greatly to the safety of the state. . . .[34]

What are 'the right ideas about things' and who decides them? This question becomes more striking, and the utopian project more sinister and illiberal, when we turn to B.F.Skinner's utopia, *Walden Two* (the publication of which postdated *News from Nowhere* by half a century). In Skinner's behaviourist experiment, which was actually established for a few years on the Twin Oaks commune in Virginia, the environment is manipulated so as to reward good and punish bad social behaviour. Between More's totalitarian schooling and Skinner's model in human manipulation, are to be found Robert Owen, the paternalistic employer whose own moral objectives were to be imposed as norms to be reached by his utopian employees; Edward Bellamy, with his nightmarish militarized labour force overlooked by an industrial officer class; and Etienne Cabet, whose Icarian school children were all to be taught from just one state-approved text book, *L'Ami des Enfants*. It is reasonable, therefore, for readers of *News from Nowhere* to question just how freely the inhabitants of Morris's utopia choose to behave as they do.

Morris accepted the basic 'theory of the perfectibility of man by the amelioration of his surroundings', [35] as expounded by Owen in his *Essays on the Formation of Character*. Owen's thesis was that 'Any general character, from the best to the worst, from the most ignorant to the most enlightened, may be given to any community, even to the world at large . . .'[36] Owen turned Augustine on his head. Unlike Morris, Owen thought that such an environment could be the product of state legislation or, failing that, benevolent employers. Morris rejected such small-scale withdrawals from capitalist society, and the underlying assumption behind them that capitalism could be eroded gradually by experimental, co-operative examples. Like Morris, Owen thought that an environment of economic wellbeing—one where human needs were properly met and labour was pleasant—

was a basic prerequisite for the development of decent, co-operative characters.

In contrast with other utopians, Morris had no plans to school or indoctrinate the children of his utopia. In Nowhere neither the dull regime of the utilitarian classroom nor the youth indoctrination of statist utopias are to be found. There are no schools in Nowhere. To be sure, the level of knowledge of Nowhere's children compares well with that of our own society, with its problem of mass illiteracy and frustrated pupils resenting pointless lessons in conformity. In Nowhere most children can read by the time they are four, and can usually speak French, German, Latin, Greek, as well as Welsh or Irish—they 'pick them up very quickly, because their elders all know them'.[37] 'Book-learning' is emphasized less than experiential study, and learning to write—'scrawl'—is considered less important than 'handsome writing'.[38] Learning does not take place in an institution, but is a living, free experience which is not compulsory, but stimulated by curiosity. Practical skills are regarded as no less worthy an aspect of learning than more abstract intellectual pursuits. Relaxed, non-regimented learning, freed from the competitive examining rituals and degrading notions of teachers and taught, comprise one of the most attractive features of Nowhere.

The absence of compulsory instruction frees Nowhere from the danger, so evident in *Utopia* and *Walden Two*, of an intellectual élite having the power to direct the people's 'habit of acting on the whole for the best'. The nurture of human decency is not an active process of moral imposition, but a passive, spontaneous response to non-competitive material conditions.

In Nowhere there are no police or prisons or courts of law. Just as there are no schools, there is no formal machinery for dealing with members of society who transgress. As for punishment, it is regarded as a foolish anachronism. Elaborating upon the theme of crime, Hammond explains that 'By far the greater part of these in past days were the result of the laws of private property, which forbade the satisfaction of their natural desires to all but a privileged few . . .'[39] Other crimes derived from other property-based relationships: for example, sexual jealousy and 'artificial perversions of the sexual passions' which arose from 'the idea (a law-made idea) of the woman being the property of the man...'[40] Other causes of crime, which are absent in Nowhere, involved the repressive restrictions of the legal family and the competitive impetus to be better than ones neighbours which had caused 'scowling envy' in a society where only some people were seen as being of value. All such 'criminal' behaviour has virtually disappeared in this new society of friends. In presenting such a challenge to the notion of innate criminal drives, Morris deviated radically from what most Victorians accepted as basic truths about human nature. Morris wrote *News from Nowhere* at a time when criminological theory was still in its relative infancy, dependent largely upon the Lombrosian fallacy of 'criminal types'. In our own time there is much greater agreement about the property basis (including broader areas of sexual and familial possessiveness) of most crimes. Few respectable students of criminal behaviour would go beyond society to seek the cause of crime: neither theological sin nor metaphysical criminal natures can be invoked as explanations for the bank robber or the insider dealer.

This is not to say that social transgressions do not occur in Nowhere. But when they do happen they are seen, both by society and by the transgressor, as 'the errors of friends, not the habitual actions of persons driven into enmity against society'.[41] In such cases society is not so insecure as to demand revenge against the wrongdoer, for if 'we torture the man, we turn his grief into anger, and the humiliation he would otherwise feel for *his* wrong-doing is swallowed up by a hope of revenge for *our* wrong-doing to him.'[42] Except for cases where they are 'sick or mad (in which case he must be restrained till his sickness or madness is cured)',[43] all that Nowhere asks of its transgressors is that they feel remorse and ask for society's pardon—which is readily given. One is a little uneasy about so-called madness being a justification for enforced restraint; Morris was writing at a time before there was widespread sensitivity to the dangers of psychiatric abuse, and before writers such as Szasz and Laing produced their radical and compelling critiques of 'the myth of mental illness'.[44] That reservation aside, is it really so absurd to envisage a society which has matured beyond the requirement for institutionalized punishment? Is it 'natural' to inflict pain upon those who transgress against our shared norms? In Victorian society it was considered quite natural for parents and teachers to beat transgressing children harshly. In our own times child-beating is outlawed in most schools and seen as a social problem when apparent in families. If we can progress in our dealing with children, from imposing humiliating anguish to teaching responsible remorse for wrongdoing, is it really beyond the horizon of plausible human behaviour to envisage a society without revenge or punishment? The account of the murder in Nowhere, and the sensitive way in which the people respond to it, provides a touching perspective upon this vision of a non-vengeful society.[45]

The absence of schools and prisons are optimistic indicators that we are looking at a refreshingly non-authoritarian utopia. But still the sceptical onlooker has a right to ask more questions before this utopian vision can be certified as a genuine accomplishment of unenforced social harmony. Central to such questioning is the matter of the freedom to dissent; it is that liberty which distinguishes harmony from totalitarianism. In St Augustine's *City of God* or Calvin's Geneva the authoritarian repression of dissent against the divine will serves to cement the unity of true believers. Even those entering Rousseau's Enlightenment-based Social Contract must accept that the General Will is entitled to force them to be free. In Nowhere cohesion is not the product of compulsion. It is not enough that the inhabitants of Nowhere should be free from the tyranny of employers and the State for them to be truly free: they must be free also from any stultifying morality which pushes minorities—even minorities of one—into the isolation of the despised dissident. Morris was emphatic about this, explaining in 1887 that 'my ideal of the Society of the future is first of all freedom and cultivation of the individual will . . .'[46] Hammond is rightly concerned to explain that the inhabitants of Nowhere are free from moral as well as legal coercion:

> . . . perhaps you will be shocked when I tell you that there is no code of public opinion which takes the place of . . . courts, and which might be as tyrannical and unreasonable as they were. I do not say that people don't judge their neighbours' conduct, sometimes, doubtless, unfairly. But I do say that there is no unvarying conventional set of rules by which people are judged;

no bed of Procrustes to stretch or cramp their crowded minds and lives; no hypocritical excommunication which people are *forced* to pronounce, either by unconsidered habit, or by the unexpressed threat of the lesser interdict if they are lax in their hypocrisy.[47]

This affirmation of the freedom of individuals to think or behave differently from those around them places Nowhere in a tradition of libertarianism from which most utopias must be excluded. In Nowhere people do not always agree with one another and can not always be persuaded to perform social functions which do not suit them.[48] Within the limits of majority rule, organized minorities are free to pursue their own particular ends, as is well demonstrated in the story of 'the obstinate refusers'.[49] One is not left with the impression that the 'habit of acting on the whole for the best' implies dull conformity, or the repression of that individual creativity which the capitalist system celebrates, but rarely fosters.

In *News from Nowhere* Morris endeavoured to depict humans as they could be. He did not suggest that only Nowhere's people were 'truly human' or even that they were more 'natural' than the Guest and the property-minded people from whom he came. Morris was too imaginative a materialist to presume to have discovered a single, finalized human nature; he understood that human behaviour— relationships, culture, feelings of self-identity—are fundamentally historical. Stripped of capitalist education, capitalist domestication, capitalist work routines, capitalist legislation and morality, Morris allowed himself to depict humans freed to behave beyond the limiting confines of the money-wages-profits system. Thus liberated, he did not seek, either in utopian vision or political practice, to impose upon humanity a new, socialist process of conditioning. To seek to organize and regiment human freedom would be to subvert human freedom; it would be to exhibit a profound lack of faith in the potentiality of unfettered humanity. The contrast between Morris's vision of an unschooled, undomesticated, non-employed, lawless, and yet reasonable and practical people, and Edward Bellamy's coerced, regimented, bureaucratized cogs in the techno-utopian machine points to two distinct theories about the relationship between social efficiency and human nature.

News from Nowhere is a vital contribution to a long-fought and far from purely academic debate about what human beings may one day become. Is human nature a barrier to the highest form of social freedom? Since the fourth century, mainstream Judeo-Christian ideology has dominated this debate; to challenge that ideology has led to being placed on the utopian margins of the history of ideas. This is not the place to address the biological, psychological, anthropological and historical complexities of the human nature debate; it was certainly not Morris's intention in *News from Nowhere* to offer a comprehensive contribution to such broad areas of thought. Morris's modest aim was to depict what co-operative humanity might look like; free, friendly, non-aggressive beings—and yet unmistakably human beings. In the century since the publication of *News from Nowhere* two world wars, concentration camps, Nazism, Stalinism, nuclear militarism, as well as the more mundane obscenities of pervasive cultural, political and environmental degradation, have done more to turn the public gaze towards an Orwell, a Huxley or a Zamiatin than to Morris. The case for humans as intelligent, social animals, capable of the most wonderful ingenuity, fellowship and joy, is all too easily frowned upon by cynics. *News from Nowhere* offers a picture of human life emancipated from the cynics' everyday fears. If it fails to convince, then that is at least in part a reflection of the intensity of the modern fear of freedom. Utopian vision alone will not remove such conservative fear; Morris was the last to think that utopia alone could do that. For Morris, vision must be combined with active striving to change the world, 'striving, with whatsoever pain and labour needs must be, to build up little by little the day of fellowship, and rest, and happiness.'[50]

❧ 4 ❧

The Obstinate Refusers:
Work in *News from Nowhere*

RAY WATKINSON

IT IS HALLIDAY SPARLING[1] who tells how once, in a discussion
with comrades, Morris suddenly picked up a copy of his *Love is
Enough*, and exclaimed 'This is a lie, and it was I who wrote it! Love
and WORK, that is what we need!' And it is in this light that we must
look at what Morris shows of work, and its place in the lives of those
who live in Nowhere. Work is presented in *News from Nowhere* as
a necessity of life, needed and hungered after. It is thus put on the
same plane as hunger, sex, and love. Hunger makes not even a ghostly
appearance in Nowhere: but sex does, and love, and work is never
far from these.

Many of those to whom the socialist propaganda was addressed,
were all too familiar with the need for work of quite another kind.
In the main, this meant a desperate need for employment, for a wage
with which to buy shelter, food and clothing for themselves and their
families. Though many of them would follow specific trades, it was
common enough in times of general unemployment, or of recession
in particular trades, for them to find themselves forced to accept, even
to plead for, work in another trade, or as labourers doing unskilled
or semi-skilled work.

Having found, in the trade to which you had been apprenticed, in
its physical skills and the intellectual activities embedded in their use,
a real source of pleasure, you might, often as not, find yourself
expected, in the interest of profit, to work too fast, or to cut corners,
skimping both materials and skill. You might be doing this in
cramped, dark, and dirty conditions, and for long hours, leaving little
time for leisure. In the hardest of times, the thing most dreaded was

that you should be forced to sell your tools for bread. From that pit there was mostly no return. This was a particular factor in the lives of those workers with whom Morris was most familiar, the skilled craft workers of the furnishing and decorative trades. In contrast, the factory hand had no place from which to fall but simply out of work into destitution, until the swing of trade, or the times, called for more workers to be once more taken on.

This was a condition of life which Morris had read about, but had not seen at first hand, the condition which offered no imagined pleasure in labour. Many of the readers of *Commonweal* could share Morris's dream: and it was his particular hope to win them away from the mechanistic pseudo-socialism of Bellamy's *Looking Backward* that first impelled him to write *News from Nowhere*. To fall out of your trade merely to survive was a blow both to self-esteem, and to *hope*. It made clear that the search for work was, in the end, not for specific employment, but for work-in-general—not as an abstraction, but as the means of access to daily bread. To learn this bitter lesson, however, opened the possibility of looking further, if hope of a change, and of some control over your own life could be found. It was to give such hope that men like Morris joined the socialist propaganda of the 1880s, and that he wrote *News from Nowhere*.

One reader of SDF and Socialist League propaganda, and who had read Morris, was Robert Noonan ('Robert Tressell'), who was personally familiar with the kind of experience described above. And nowhere is the pressure and the degradation forced upon those actually in work more vividly expressed than in *The Ragged-Trousered Philanthropists*,[2] which is set in Morris's own trade of decoration. There is a parallel to be drawn between Noonan himself, his own 'hero' Owen, and the nameless 'hero' of Morris's *The Pilgrims of Hope*, which had preceded *News from Nowhere* in the pages of *The Commonweal*.

The Pilgrims of Hope is far from being as well-known, or as much studied as it should be: it is a serious text of socialist thought. Here, the skilled man, a joiner by trade, is secure in the workshop because of his skill; but also, and in the end more so, because he has a small 'private' income. The self-confidence that this, and a better education than most of his fellows, gives, wins him respect from them, and keeps the boss off his back. The moment an absconding lawyer brings the income to an abrupt end, the boss takes him to task for his subversive views, and his street corner speaking. Soon, skill, education and all, he is 'on the stones', and reduced to the basic condition of the industrial worker, which is not that of being *in* work, but of being *available* for work, a commodity on the labour market.[3]

Work in Nowhere

Work, in *News from Nowhere*, is not often described circumstantially, though this Morris could well have done: his intention was not a mechanical account of technical matters, such as Bellamy might have offered, but an evocation of relationships, all of which at some point have work as an element, though it may not be, most of the time, in central focus. As Guest and Dick the boatman drive gently from Hammersmith towards Bloomsbury, Guest lights the pretty pipe he has just a little while before obtained from a shop (to his bewilderment, without payment). His comments on the fine carving of the bowl give an opportunity for a few words from Dick on carving in general.

> Of course, if carvers were scarce, they would all be busy on the architecture, as you call it, and then these 'toys' (a good word) would not be made; but since there are plenty of people who can carve . . . in fact, almost everybody, and as the work is somewhat scarce, or we are afraid it might be, folk do not discourage this kind of petty work.[4]

Guest is about to enter into a difficult discussion of what is valuable, when he sees that they are passing a big building, in which some sort of work seemed to be going on. This Dick explains as a 'Banded Workshop' in which people come to work together—in this instance, at pottery and glass-making, to make use of common facilities. 'It must be the power that brings them,' Guest suggests. 'Why so?' says Dick: 'they can have power at home or wherever they like: it is the big kilns and other equipment, and above all the companionship, that draw them.' No smoke comes from the furnaces. 'Smoke?' says Dick.

'Why should you see smoke?'[5]—and as in the case of the 'force-barges' seen on the river, and the equivalent road vehicles, Guest realizes that here is a scientific development which he does not understand, and thinks best not to enquire into. Morris was probably thinking of electricity, by then well-developed, and beginning to have industrial uses, as many of his readers would know from daily experience. But technology is not the point: how people live together, what work means to them, how all the beauty of their buildings and ornament has come about (he is never taken to meet artists in their studios, still less architects or writers)—these are the matter of Morris's argument.

The way into this scene is both innocent and significant. Our introduction to work in the story is at the very beginning, with Dick waiting in his boat for the first would-be swimmer—who is the bewildered Morris of last-night's Socialist League. Since he cannot pay Dick for his rowing, and finds that he is anyway about to relinquish the job to a friend, as a favour, it does not look at all like work as he has known it in his 'real' world. Nor does the friendly and easy serving of breakfast in the guest house seem more like such work: yet these people use the word, and the things they do are useful and necessary.

Presently, they come upon a gang of men road-mending

... which delayed us a little; but I was not sorry for it; for all I had hitherto seen seemed a mere part of a summer holiday; and *I wanted to see how this folk would set to a piece of real necessary work.*[6] [my italics]

The gang consists of about a dozen

strong young men, looking much like a boating party at Oxford would have looked ... and not more troubled with their work ... a half-dozen of young women stood by watching the work or the workers, both of which were worth watching. . . . They were laughing and talking merrily with each other and the women.[7]

They have chosen this necessary piece of public work because they are well able to do it, with all the will and the pleasure of a rowing team, and because it needs to be done. As Guest looks, the gang stops work to make way for their vehicle, and helps the old horse by easing the wheels over the half-undone road. This image, and the reference to Oxford, readily reminds us of Ruskin's road-building at Hinksey, and Morris would know this: but these are not privileged young gentlemen: simply a gang doing a job. There is another and more important reference here: to Ford Madox Brown's painting *Work* (1852-1863).

If Morris's brief word-picture is less packed with detail and particular meanings than *Work*, it must be understood in the light of that painting, which in the 1850s was a direct statement of fact, but pointing no way forward, as now did Morris, in *News from Nowhere*. In *Work*, every figure is individual: each of the navvies is both type and person—within the powerful collective entity of the gang. Though the two most conspicuous stand in heroic attitudes, it is the gang, not any of its members, that is the hero; and the gang is an image of the working class. The other figures, too, appear in relation to this working group; they are, all but the wandering herb-gatherer separated in his dream, middle class.

Brown was working on this painting when, early in his first days in London, Morris, newly friendly with Rossetti, was taken to see him: it would be in his studio, being elaborated, while Morris worked there under Brown's guidance on his first commissioned but long-lost painting *Tristram recognized by the Dog he had given Iseult*. Morris offers, in *News from Nowhere*, a very different image of work, of the road gang, of their relationships with passers-by and onlookers: one, naturally, far less-detailed in every way than Brown's in his painting: but the comparison is valuable.

Painting *Work* had brought Brown to a new strong sympathy with working men. In his search for models—who must not just be recognizable as labourers, but each show a distinct type—he talked to a great many; came to know some very well, and learn from them about their lives. One of them, five or six years later, became a packer for Morris, Marshall, Faulkner & Co., when Morris, Brown, and their friends, set up that important little communal enterprise. Morris, in writing his little picture of the road gang, could not fail to remember Brown's painting, and his early debt to the painter, not only for teaching, but for earnest conversations on social issues. Both he and Brown had married working-class wives: Jane Morris's father was a groom, Emma Brown's a building worker. Nor could he fail to recall the years of anger and resentment that had kept him and Brown apart after the recasting of The Firm in 1875 as Morris & Co.

The old, deep friendship of thirty years before could never be as it had been, but in 1884, in his early days as socialist propagandist, Morris had been reconciled to Brown by the act of a Manchester SDF member, a joiner who did work for Brown, then painting his murals in Manchester Town Hall. Brown, in youth a radical liberal, as Morris had been, was never a member of a political party, and took rather a Proudhonist stance. In his early Hampstead days, at the time of the painting of *Work*, and *The Last of England*, he had set up a soup-kitchen: and in the eighties in Manchester did the same. While he would always steer clear of any organization such as the SDF or the Socialist League, he was much in sympathy with Morris's open political agitation, and subscribed to *The Commonweal*.

Technology

Why does Morris show only manual work in *News from Nowhere*, which, whatever it may have of subjectivity, is not simply about projecting the work and conditions of Morris & Co. on to our whole future? It is not because his utopia uses no machinery. In more than one place he indicates very clearly that machinery is used, and that new sources of power, probably electricity, are in general use. Thus, during Guest's journey up the Thames with Clara and Dick, we read that

> Both on this day, as well as yesterday, we had, as you may think, met and passed and been passed by, many craft of one kind or another. The most part of these were being rowed like ourselves, or were sailing, in the sort of way that sailing is managed on the upper reaches of the river; but every now and then we came on barges, laden with hay or other country produce, or carrying bricks, lime, timber, and the like, and these were going on their way without any means of propulsion visible to me . . . just a man at the tiller, with often a friend or two laughing and talking with him. Dick, seeing on one occasion that I was looking hard

at one of these, said: 'That is one of our force-barges; it is quite
as easy to work vehicles by force by water as by land.' I understood pretty well that these 'force vehicles' had taken the place
of our old steam-power carrying; but I took good care not to ask
any questions about them.[8]

and as they near Kelmscott, Ellen, who has now joined them, says,
just after they have passed a mill

'You seem astonished at this being so pleasant to look at!' . . . I
should have said that all along the Thames were an abundance
of mills used for various purposes; none of which were in any
degree unsightly, and many strikingly beautiful: and the gardens
about them marvels of loveliness.[9]

Nor are these machines seen as alien, for he is explicit, in the
account of the Banded Workshop at Bloomsbury, that people may
have power to use not only in such large, communal enterprises, but
at home, individually. Power here is to be taken as for machine or
for process. And in discussion of machinery, Old Hammond makes
it clear that it is, and should be, available to do those things that cannot be done, or done so well, by hand, or are excessively laborious,
tedious, repetitive or repulsive.[10]

At Wallingford, Guest, Clara and Dick stop to eat, and meet an
elderly man, Henry Morsom, 'who seemed in a country way to be
another edition of Hammond'.[11] He tells them much about local history, including Civil War episodes: but as much about the change
from machinery to hand work; how after the breakdown of production in the later Civil War, which made possible the communism
under which they now live, it had been necessary to learn again how
the machines worked, how to make, maintain, repair, even how to
reinvent them, in order to get the economy moving again; and even,
as the town populace moved out into the country, how to learn handi-
crafts by studying them, function by function, so analysing machines
as to work back to the hand-actions which they had been invented
to take over under power.

What Morris is against is not the machines, but the alienation that,
under capitalism, they produce. Thus,

You must remember that the handicraft was not the result of what used to be called material necessity: on the contrary, by that time the machines had been so much improved that almost all necessary work might have been done by them: and indeed, many people at that time, and before it, used to think that machinery would entirely supersede handicraft, which certainly, on the face of it, seemed more than likely. But there was another opinion, far less logical, prevalent among the rich people before the days of freedom, which did not die out at once after that epoch had begun. This opinion, which from all I can learn, seemed as natural then as it seems absurd now, was, that while the ordinary daily work of the world would be done entirely by automatic machinery, the energies of *the more intelligent part of mankind* would be set free to follow the higher forms of art, as well as science and the study of history. It was strange, was it not, that they should ignore that aspiration after complete equality which we now recognise as the bond of all happy human society.[12]

Clara's comment is that this attitude arose from the general view of human life as separate from that of all other life.

It was natural to people thinking in this way, that they should try to make nature their slave, since they thought 'nature' was something outside them.[13]

And thus the majority of humans also began to be treated as objects to be exploited.

Morris not only hates the alienation between humans which comes from and gives rise to exploitation, but sees that the actual use of machinery, as well as its applications, may itself be alienating. In craft cultures, by no means free of exploitation, the implement was an extension of the intelligent hand, and in no way alienating, in no way destructive of the 'sensuous' element necessary to the pleasure of work. Under the pressure of the market, in the pursuit of unlimited production, the implement itself is taken beyond that point to become a machine, severing the sensuous link, reducing the function of the intelligent hand, taking away the control of the workers' intuitive acts, reducing the workers, as the machine develops to its own perfection, to minders and servants—alienated in their work, and alienated in society by this degradation as they become less important than the machine they serve. All this is not in the interest of making the object of use or beauty, but in making the commodity saleable on the widest market, and at the least, but most profitable, cost.

No doubt, in his earliest approaches to this problem, Morris saw it in romantic, anti-modern terms, in the light of Ruskin's teaching: and it probably took him a long time to discard this romantic hostility to the machine as such, and to come to terms with the social aspects of machine production, to recognise that there are indeed uses for machines which might really be what was so often pretended in capitalist society, 'labour saving'—this depending on social control, free of exploitive interests and the profit motive.

I do not think that Morris modified his views on the use of machinery simply by adjusting theory to the needs of his socialist convictions and propaganda: I think that the change in his outlook, though slow and reluctant, went hand in hand with his way of life, and that between 1871 and 1875, against the background of the breakdown of his relationship with Jane; his increasingly important role in the management of The Firm, leading at last to its rebirth as Morris & Co, and the part which he chose, in those same years, to exercise in the affairs of the Devon Great Consolidated Mine Company, all played their part in deepening his understanding of economic and social affairs. Long a radical liberal, he began to see that more than general adherence to reforming sentiments was needed.

Devon Great Consols had always been very much a family concern: the Morrises were not the only shareholders, but William Morris senior had held, and left to his wife and children, about one fifth of the stake: his brother Thomas had from the beginning been the managing partner in Tavistock, and another brother also had shares. Emma Morris had arranged for each of her children on coming of age to receive a proportion of the inheritance: what Morris did in this respect therefore—and he was head of the family—affected all his brothers and sisters, and their mother. It was to deal with this that in 1871, he became a director, and remained so until 1875.

In 1876, he turned his whole attention to what had become, in March 1875, Morris & Company. He had used some of his Devon Great Consols shares to capitalize the new concern, and, mindful of his family duties, had sold them to his younger brother Stanley, who took his place on the Board. By this time too (1874), Rossetti had had a second severe crisis: had left Kelmscott Manor for good, and ceased to be Janey's lover. In every way, 1875 was the great divide between Morris's first life and his new one, and this meant it was also the beginning of his move into socialism.

Beyond Ruskin

It is not first or most to *News from Nowhere* that we should look for a full statement of Morris's ideas on art and work, though the measure of their identity is central to the book—expressed more in terms of relationships than of the production of things. This is characteristic of *News from Nowhere*, and it was to explore the transformation of relationships such as should follow the establishment of a socialist commonwealth (the very thing which Bellamy's book missed) that Morris, enraged by a picture of social life 'after the revolution' as a cross between a barracks and a department store, set out to do. We can learn something of his matured ideas on this his lifelong dream, from *News from Nowhere*, but it is more fruitful, and the specific evidence stronger, if we take it back to much earlier days, and show how, out of his own life-experience, he came by stages to the vision implicit in *News from Nowhere*. These are set out more fully and specifically in some lectures, of which the first is the one that he gave to the Trades Guild of Learning on 4th December 1877—his first formal public utterance.[14] Little attention has been given to this shadowy body,[15] and it was not the only factor in the development of Morris's ideas about art. It was though, important, and Morris's involvement marks a step forward from his Ruskinian beginnings to a new stage.

We might in fact set out Morris's development from his innocent romantic beginnings, to his settled views, helped to coherence by his reading of Marx, and his part in the socialist propaganda of the eighties. The age of innocence begins when a naif, antiquarian, quasi-religious and medievalising idea finds its first expression in the poems, stories and articles of the *Oxford and Cambridge Magazine* (1856). The articles rest very much, and consciously, on Ruskin: of whom he had read (before the magazine was published) *Modern Painters* volumes I and II; *The Seven Lamps of Architecture*; the Edinburgh Lectures, and, supreme, *The Stones of Venice*, and out of '*Stones*', the famous chapter on 'The Nature of Gothic Architecture and of the true office of the workman in Art'.[16] That is already a good deal, and the best of Ruskin, and in Morris's view, as he reminded the world with his reprinting of that chapter at the Kelmscott Press in 1892, the most important. It is to be remarked that in his foreword to that reprint[17] he is at pains to link it with *Unto This Last*[18] of 1862, and the articles published by Ruskin in *Fraser's Magazine*,[19] which herald the Marxist account of the relations between labour and capital and production which Morris came to know twenty years later.

Morris read with great eagerness all that Ruskin wrote, at least up to *Fors Clavigera*:[20] after that, perhaps he troubled less not only about what Ruskin might say about art (the last volumes of *Modern Painters* he called 'mostly gammon'), but about society too, for by 1870 Ruskin's overstretched mind was in increasing disorder and distress. But if we recognize how exciting and how important to him was this reading—almost certainly at the instigation of Frederick Barlow Guy, his tutor between Marlborough and Oxford—we should also recognize that these books were all part of his coming to maturity, and entering the world from which to so large an extent his upbringing had sheltered him. Morris himself says, in the preface to the Kelmscott Press reprint of 'The Nature of Gothic' that, important as Ruskin's ideas on painting had been—the only light shining in the darkness of that time—it was his ideas on social order and morality that, in the end, were his most valuable contribution to the age. And Ruskin himself thought that the chapter was the most important part of the *Stones of Venice*. In writing it, he had opened up a new world of ideas.

With the Edinburgh lectures, which Morris and his friends read on first publication, Ruskin began a frontal assault on the civic pride and the complacency of the solid Scottish middle class from which he came: and a few years later, in 1859, the great wave of building strikes and lockouts, especially in London, disturbed him deeply, provoking him to a new look at modern labour relations and social justice. When Thackeray launched the *Cornhill Magazine* in 1860,

Ruskin published four new, short, simply phrased papers, in which he set out the ideas he had been pondering. Written in unidealistic and rational terms, they deeply disturbed his Tory parents, and so incensed the mainly Whig readers of the magazine that Thackeray had to bring them to an abrupt end. They appeared in a small volume two years later under the biblical title *Unto This Last*.[21] This Morris read, and in the preface to the Kelmscott edition of 'The Nature of Gothic', says of it

> that great book *Unto This Last*, which has had the most enduring and beneficent effect on his contemporaries, and will have through them on succeeding generations.[22]

In 'The Nature of Gothic', Ruskin divides human activities into four types of *Play*. These are: *wise* play; *necessary* play; *inordinate* play; and *not playing at all*; the unhappy few in this last kind being 'so dull or morose as to be incapable of inventing or jest'.[23] This takes Ruskin into a discussion of the Grotesque as an area in which the workers in the Gothic world, laboriously employed, found outlets for their perceptions and inventions.

> For one hard-working man who possesses the finer instincts which decide on perfection of lines and harmonies of colour, twenty possess dry humour or quiet fancy; not because these facilities were originally given to the human race, or to any section of it, in greater degree than the sense of beauty, but because these are exercised in our daily intercourse with each other, and developed by the interest we take in the affairs of life, while the others do not. . . . We have seen that (the workman's) application to art is to be playful and recreative, and it is not in recreation that the conditions of perfection can be fulfilled.[24]

Most obviously it was the carved bosses and corbels, the story-telling enrichments of doorways, the misericordes, that showed this play, but Ruskin, and Morris following him as well as his own perceptions, would include the tender playfulness of the carved capitals and crockets, the diapered infillings in blank arches,—all, the sweetest or the most grotesque, drawn by the workers from the living world about them as they worked, and not set out for them with rule and compass by master mason or architect.

Morris's first published story, in the January number of the *Oxford and Cambridge Magazine* of 1856, the 'Story of the Unknown Church',[25] makes great play of exactly this freedom. It is present too in the last two stanzas of that best-known of the poems of *The Defence of Guenevere*, 'Concerning Geffraye Teste Noir',[26] which may have been drafted at the same time. Central to each is the building and carving of a shrine to dead lovers, and the character of the carving is of free invention. Necessary play was, from the beginning, an essential part of Morris's gothic vision, and we must expect to find it in *News from Nowhere* too. And indeed we do: for instance in the illustration of what shopping means, the new pipe Guest is given for his old, lost corncob, and the splendid carved friezes Guest has already seen in the Dining Hall and the Moot Hall of Hammersmith.

Red House, Work, and News from Nowhere

Eldest son of a large family, Morris had avoided the Church, stepping sideways into architecture, then just resolving itself into a profession. From this, within a year, he had moved on to an untramelled artist's life: marrying and becoming the owner of a house built to accommodate his family and to express his ideas; to become, at the age of forty, sole proprieter and master, as well as chief designer and mastercraftsman, of an active company of a hundred workers of different kinds—all of whom, from shop boy to manager, were his employees.

This was not necessarily Morris's original intention for his life, or The Firm. I am convinced that at Red House, and in workshops immediately at hand, Morris meant to set up a small enterprise for the making of decorative goods such as architects might commission for churches, public buildings, or big private houses. This enterprise would be small in scale, and simple in its aims, would not employ many workers, nor be seen in managerial terms. Rather than those of employer and employees in trade, relationships would have been personal, familial and the kind experienced with house servants— those written of by Ruskin in his 'Roots of Honour'.[27] The contrast with Devon Great Consols, which in its time was the greatest copper mine in the world, with some forty miles of underground levels, and on which some six thousand people depended for their living,[28] could not have been greater.

Red House would have been something different from The Firm: it would have been a 'Banded Workshop' such as is described thirty years later in *News from Nowhere*:[29] where a number of like-minded people, wishing to carry on certain kinds of work which will be better done thereby, come together in one building or set of buildings, with suitable equipment and facilities. In Nowhere there is no Boss: at Red House there would always have been Morris, but working on a familial basis with Ned (Burne-Jones), Jane, Georgie (Georgiana Burne-Jones) at least as equals, others with standing much more of that of family servants. There is, of course, in Nowhere, a ganger who organizes the work of the road-menders, but hardly as a boss, in no way proprietorial or managerial.

Morris's situation at The Firm, whether at Red Lion Square, or Queen Square, was never quite what he had meant; inevitably and especially as so much work was in his hands, he had much more the position of boss or manager; perhaps more so after 1870, when George Wardle took over as manager from Warington Taylor. Taylor, son of wealthy gentry, ex-officer and Old Etonian, saw himself as the equal of the partners: Wardle could never do this, and deferred much more to Morris. In the end, though, he became so valuable as to encourage Morris in his next step, the takeover of The Firm, which at last freed him to do what he meant for Red House some fifteen years before.

The important token of this is that the first thing Morris had Wardle do, once severance was complete, and The Firm safely Morris & Company, was to draw up a profit-sharing scheme, which Morris then adopted virtually unaltered. It is this scheme which in 1884 he described in fair detail to Georgie:[30] he knows it is not socialism: he knows it is not the way to solve the problems of capitalist society: it is what he can do within that society while running The Firm on as egalitarian a basis as he can, doing his own large and multiple work within, making public propaganda for the necessary new order.

When he thought of setting up Red House as that 'banded workshop' he did not envisage a workforce of a hundred—that would not have been feasible—but it is in keeping with the same Ruskinian plan that he never let his workforce much exceed a hundred, nor did it ever fall much below: stability, wages above the market, one or two old employees no longer able to work significantly found possible tasks, and kept on—with mutual respect.

Conclusions

Ruskin lays the foundation of Morris's ideas: Marx crowns them, and Morris gladly acknowledged both debts while taking the ideas further. Ruskin could not propose any change in the existing social order, though *Unto This Last* sets out plainly its unjust and alienating character. He can only propose self-denying ordinances and conscientious dealing between people within the given heirarchies, central to which shall be mutual respect between masters and men.

Morris, like the angry readers of *Fraser's* and the *Cornhill*, saw where Ruskin's stark analysis must lead, though he despaired of seeing how change might come. From 1875, he was in no doubt that change must come, and set himself to find out what was to be done. From 1883, he was clear about Socialism, and the need for revolutionary change, not mere amelioration. For him, therefore, travelling beyond Ruskin, the matter of the interpenetration of art and work, comes to be seen not only in the existing context, but in the projected context of an egalitarian society in which alone they can be reunited.

In his Hammersmith workroom, designing, writing poetry, he hears with rage the rowdy passing drunks—rage not that his quiet is disturbed, but that society should so degrade its children. He reflects on his own good fortune, not in money terms—which had given him freedom to choose—but as a matter of art and work. For the poor, worker and unemployed alike, these are polar opposites. For him, ever since his decision to enter Street's office, they have been mutually necessary elements in a fulfilled life, and he is outraged that such a life is denied to the great majority of people—and not only to the poor.

Once he had seen, romantically, Art as our salvation. Now he sees, as he writes the first instalment of *News from Nowhere* for *The Commonweal*, that art itself must be saved, and that only by saving work—and those who perform it—from the alienation and degradation imposed by industrial capitalism, can either work, or art, and thus living society, be made fully human for all.

෨ 5 ෧

Concerning Love:
News from Nowhere and Gender

JAN MARSH

DURING THE 1880s–90s, the 'Woman Question' was as lively
an issue as Feminism in the 1980s–90s, permeating all areas of
discussion, not least those of the socialist movement. However radical their views on the transformation of society through class struggle, many socialists held traditional views on the present and future
position of women, whereas it was precisely the promise of an entirely
re-structured way of life that attracted to the cause many articulate,
active women who questioned and challenged all the prescriptions
and restrictions of prevailing gender ideology. As a leading lecturer
and propagandist of the Socialist League, William Morris was unav-
oidably drawn into the debate, and his responses to feminist issues
are an important and even dominant element in *News from Nowhere*.

In *The Origin of the Family, Private Property and the State*, first
published in 1884, Friedrich Engels offered a Marxist analysis of the
Woman Question, tracing patriarchal oppression to its ancient roots,
claiming that in the 'savage' and 'barbarous' stages of human history,
'the position of woman [was] not only free but honourable', family
life taking the form of group marriage in a society of primitive communism, with 'mother-right' or matriarchal authority and lines of
descent. With the rise of civilization and private ownership, however,

the overthrow of mother-right was the *world historical defeat*
of the female sex. The man took command in the house also; the
woman was degraded and reduced to servitude, she became the
slave of his lust and a mere instrument for the production of his
children.[1] [Original italics]

The first class opposition in history, that of owners/ bosses versus serfs/workers, Engels continued, coincides with the development of antagonism between male and female in patriarchal marriage, and 'the first class oppression coincides with that of the female sex by the male'.

Through the classical, feudal and capitalist epochs this pattern persists. In bourgeois marriage, the woman 'sells her body once and for all into slavery'. In Protestant countries, the sale is disguised by the element of free choice allowed to each spouse, but the usual result is 'a conjugal partnership of leaden boredom known as domestic bliss. As a result, prostitution flourishes. Among the working class, free choice and true 'sex-love' is possible, since no property enters the equation and, as an equal, working partner, the wife retains the right to dissolve an unsatisfactory union.

From this rather rosy view of proletarian marriage, Engels moved on to the conditions for change:

> In the old communistic household, which comprised many couples and their children, the task entrusted to the women of managing the household was as much a public and socially necessary industry as the procuring of food by the men . . .
>
> . . . the first condition for the liberation of the wife is to bring the whole female sex back into public industry, and that in turn demands the abolition of the monogamous family as the economic unit of society.[2]

Now the proposed abolition of monogamy was one of the most alarming aspects of the Socialist movement according to its opponents, who were even more agitated by the idea of 'free love' and sexual autonomy than by the prospect of dispossessed factory-owners and landlords. As with the endorsement of gay rights today, it also alarmed many within the movement, fearful of the deterrent effect on potential supporters.

'We are now approaching a social revolution in which the economic foundations of monogamy will disappear,' Engels stated boldly. 'Will monogamy therefore disappear?' On the contrary, he responded, it will be realized completely . . . the overthrow of capitalism will bring marriage based on true sexual love and inclination . . . if affection definitely comes to an end, or is supplanted by a new passionate love, separation is a benefit for both partners as well as society—only people will then be spared having to wade through the useless mire of a divorce case . . .[3]

He ended with a hopeful, if vague, view of the future:

What can we now conjecture about the way in which sexual relations will be ordered after the impending overthrow of capitalist production? ... What will there be new? That will be answered when a new generation has grown up: a generation of men who have never in their lives known what it was to buy a woman's surrender with money or any other social instrument of power; a generation of women who have never known what it is to give themselves to a man from any other considerations than real love, or to refuse to give themselves to their lover for fear of the economic consequences. When these people are in the world, they will care precious little what anybody today thinks they ought to do; they will make their own practice and their corresponding public opinion about the practice of each individual— and that will be the end of it.[4]

These and similar views shaped socialist thinking on gender relations in the 1880s. The decade also saw the publication of August Bebel's *Woman under Socialism*, reviewed by Eleanor Marx in *The Commonweal* in April 1885 when it was translated into English as *Woman in the Past, Present and Future*. In this, the social relations of the sexes under socialism are defined as those of absolute equality—the 'equal duty of all to labour, without distinction of sex' for the general good, in an industrial system where 'everybody decides for himself [sic] in which branch he desires to be employed'. The woman receives the same education as the man, and

having performed her share of social labour in some branch of industry, the next hour she becomes educator, teacher or nurse, later on she devotes herself to art or science and afterwards exercises some executive function. She enjoys amusements and recreations with her own sex or with men, exactly as she pleases and occasion offers.

In terms of personal relations,

> in the choice of love she is free just as man is free. She wooes and is wooed and has no other inducement to bind herself than her own free will . . . the gratification of the sexual impulse is as strictly the personal affair of the individual. . . . Should incompatibility, disappointment and dislike ensue, morality demands the dissolution. . . . As men and women will be fairly equal in number . . . men will no longer be in a position to assert any superiority . . .
> Woman is therefore entirely free and her household and children, if she has any, cannot restrict her freedom but only increase her pleasure in life. Educators, friends, young girls [sic] are at hand for all cases in which she needs help.[5]

These ideas were further aired in articles and a pamphlet written by Eleanor Marx and Edward Aveling in 1885–6 'to explain the position of Socialists in respect to the woman question', in which the future perspective is sketched out:

> Clearly there will be equality for all, without distinction of sex. Thus woman will be independent: her education and all other opportunities as those of man. Like him she, if sound in mind and body (and how the number of women thus will grow!) will have to give her one, two or three hours of social labour to supply the wants of the community and therefore of herself. Thereafter she will be free for art or science or teaching or writing or amusement in any form. Prostitution will have vanished with the economic conditions that make it a necessity . . .[6]

In this context, the Woman Question was important enough for a clause on marriage to be included in the manifesto of the Socialist League, which William Morris helped to found at the beginning of 1885. But debate continued. Were legal marriage and monogamy to be abolished? In March Morris told Bernard Shaw privately that 'we of the s.l. must before long state our views on wedlock quite plainly and take the consequences, which I admit are likely to be serious'.

But the issue was complex:

> Of course I agree that abolishing wedlock while the present
> economical slavery lasts would be futile: nor do I consider a man
> a Socialist at all who is not prepared to admit the equality of
> women as far as condition goes. Also that as long as women are
> compelled to marry for a livelihood, real marriage is a rare excep-
> tion and prostitution or a kind of legalized rape the rule.[7]

Later in the year a revised manifesto for the League, which Morris
was involved in drafting, amplified the clause on sexual relations:

> Under a Socialistic system contracts between individuals would
> be voluntary and unenforced by the community. This would
> apply to the marriage contract as to others, and it would become
> a matter of simple inclination. Women also would share in the
> certainty of livelihood which would be the lot of all; and children
> would be treated from their birth as members of the community
> entitled to share in all its advantages.[8]

But such noble pronouncements obscured some of the argument, and
the same period saw an angry debate in the s.l. occasioned by an
egregious attack on sexual equality and female suffrage by Morris's
friend and collaborator Belfort Bax, defending patriarchal authority
and even marital violence. As editor of *The Commonweal*, Morris
strove to mediate, replying to one critic that 'there is more to be said
on Bax's side than you suppose ... it would be a poor economy setting
women to do men's work (as unluckily they often do now) or vice
versa.[9]

II

When, therefore, Morris sat down to write *News from Nowhere* in
1890, after the 'brisk conversational discussion as to what should
happen on the Morrow of the Revolution' in which no one listened
to anyone else's opinion and he himself 'finished by roaring out very
loud and damning all the rest for fools', he was conscious that questions of gender equality and personal relations formed a large element
in the debate about the socialist future. Indeed, it looks as if in his

'chapters from a Utopian Romance' Morris set out not only to discuss utopian economics and landscapes, but equally importantly to respond to Engels' rhetorical questions, in conjecturing 'the way in which sexual relations will be ordered . . . when a new generation has grown up', and imagining a new society for the 21st century, in which 'there will be equality for all, without distinction of sex'.

So, after the narrator William Guest first meets Dick and Robert, the handsome young waterman and the weaver, they enter the Hammersmith Guest House to be greeted by three young women who are 'at least as good as the gardens, the architecture and the male men'. (Morris is here, incidentally, aiming at non-sexist language, using 'men' in the generic sense of 'persons', as when in his correspondence he occasionally used the terms 'male-man' and 'female-man' for men and women.[10]) Firstly, the women are attractively dressed, 'decently veiled with drapery and not bundled up with millinery'; they are 'clothed like women not upholstered arm-chairs, as most women of our time are'. Moreover,

> They were so kind and happy-looking in expression of face, so shapely and well-knit of body, and thoroughly healthy-looking and strong. All were at least comely, and one of them very handsome and regular of feature. They came up to us at once and merrily and without the least affectation of shyness, and all three shook hands with me.[11]

The women lead the men to breakfast and wait on them. While one arranges a great bunch of cottage-garden roses, another brings new-picked strawberries; for thanks, Robert pats her head in a kindly manner.

So far, so disappointing, at least to feminists in the 20th century. Furthermore, the utopian quality of Nowhere is specifically confirmed a page later in terms of its effect on women's looks. When the narrator guesses that Annie, the prettiest of the three women, is twenty years of age, she replies: 'I am well served out for fishing for compliments, since I have to tell you the truth, to wit, that I am forty-two'. At this the narrator stares,

> for there was not a careful line on her face; her skin was as smooth as ivory, her cheeks full and round, her lips as red as the roses

she had brought in; her beautiful arms which she had bared for her work, firm and well-knit from shoulder to wrist. She blushed a little under my gaze, though it was clear that she had taken me for a man of eighty.[12]

As he is in fact fifty-six, the preservative qualities of Nowhere are evidently gender-free, but the main impact is on the women, whose good looks are repeatedly stressed.

Beauty, pretty clothes and the domestic graces of hospitality, flower arranging and food preparation—if these are the lineaments of utopian femininity then it is hardly surprising that, in general, women are less likely than men to find *News from Nowhere* a fully compelling vision of perfection—or even a place in which they would like to dwell. For as this early chapter demonstrates, it offers a too-masculine viewpoint, conjuring a harmonious world of decorative, contented women and active, interesting men. Dick and Robert, for example, in the space of a few lines, sketch in the breadth of their activities: sculling, silversmithing, haymaking, travelling, weaving, printing, mathematics and historical research. Each has several occupations, and scope for many more. By contrast, although not over-worked by her hotel duties at the Guest House, Annie looks forward only to reading a 'pretty old book'. This is scarcely the stuff of socialist dreams for most female readers.

Moreover, the narrator's words are those of quite unreformed masculine desire. Annie is erotically presented: feeling the warmth of Guest's sexuality, despite his age, she blushes under his gaze.

The children of Nowhere, in the following chapter, appear to enjoy a non-sexist education. They all learn, without schools or systematic teaching, and spend the summers camping in the woods, looking after themselves. But when, on their journey into central London, Dick and Guest come upon a road-mending gang, all its members are men. Their strenuous, enjoyable work and cheerful fellowship are not shared by the half-dozen young women who watch admiringly. The traditional division of labour seen at Hammersmith thus seems to be general, even natural.

Nevertheless, when in Chapters IX to XVI the various aspects of government, economics, culture and international relations are outlined through Guest's questions to old Hammond, the first inquiry relates to gender. 'Now may I ask you about the position of women in your society?' says Guest. In reply Hammond laughs, dismissing 'the emancipation of women movement' in the 19th century as a 'dead controversy'. For in the 21st century

> the men have no longer any opportunity of tyrannising over the women, or the women over the men. . . . The women do what they can do best, and what they like best, and the men are neither jealous of it or injured by it.[13]

The issue of women's suffrage—a major plank of Victorian feminism—is also irrelevant. In Nowhere there is no legislation and no Parliament and therefore no votes for women or men. But Guest persists:

> very well, then . . . but what about this woman question? I saw at the Guest House that the women were waiting on the men: that seems a little like reaction, doesn't it?

'Perhaps you think housekeeping an unimportant occupation, not deserving of respect?' retorts Hammond acerbically. 'I believe that was the opinion of the advanced women of the 19th century and their male backers.' His view is his author's:

> Don't you know that it is a great pleasure to a clever woman to manage a house skilfully, and to do it so that all the house-mates about her look pleased and are grateful to her? And then, you know, everybody likes to be ordered about by a pretty woman: why it is one of the pleasantest forms of flirtation . . .[14]

Ignoring for the moment the second, unemancipated sentence, it could be argued that here Morris is at least taking housework seriously; as Hammond says, he certainly does not subscribe to the silly notion current among the cultivated classes of 'ignoring all the steps by which their daily dinner was reached as matters too low for their lofty intelligences'. But although both Hammond and Guest claim to be good cooks (as we know Morris was, incidentally), they do not tell us that the men of Nowhere take an equal share of the domestic arts and chores: just as the men choose roadmending, so in 'doing what they like best' the women naturally enjoy housework.

Even if housework has high status, this gendered division of tasks is not what socialist feminists would regard as utopian. It has indeed, more in common with Engels' view of 'primitive communism' in which household management is as socially necessary as hunting and in which, he claimed, there was much more real respect for women than under European capitalism where

> the lady of civilization, surrounded by false homage and estranged from all real work, has an infinitely lower social position than the hard-working woman of barbarism, who was regarded among her people as a real lady.[15]

From his passion for archaic Nordic literature, we know that Morris held much the same view.

Hammond also goes on to demolish an idea proffered by Guest as the view of certain 'superior' women in his own time, who 'wanted to emancipate the more intelligent part of their sex from the bearing of children', by insisting that this folly was the result of class tyranny. In the society of the future, maternity is highly honoured. Childbirth is an extra stimulus to affection between couples, and in a land of equal access to wealth, mothers are spared sordid economic anxieties and artificial burdens, as well as the curses of heredity, which have, over time, been carefully eliminated. As a result

> the ordinarily healthy woman (and almost all our women are both healthy and at least comely) respected as a child bearer and rearer of children, desired as a woman, loved as a companion, unanxious for the future of her children, has far more instinct for maternity than the poor drudge and mother of drudges of past days could ever have; or than her sister of the upper classes, brought up in affected ignorance of natural facts, reared in an atmosphere of mingled prudery and prurience.[16]

III

Questions concerning women are thus the first to be asked and answered in *News from Nowhere*, taking precedence over those of politics and economics. They are prompted by the appearance of Clara, one of the central characters in the story, whose relationship with Dick illustrates what may be called the Marxian view of marriage and divorce, albeit with a happy resolution.

Clara and Dick were once married, or at least lived together and had two children before, in old Hammond's words

> she got it into her head that she was in love with somebody else. So she left poor Dick . . . but it did not last long . . . and then she came to me and asked how Dick was, and whether he was happy and all the rest of it.[17]

As Dick has not found another mate, all is set for a reconciliation. 'Ah,' comments Guest sagely, 'no doubt you wanted to keep them out of the Divorce Court.' But of course there are no courts in Nowhere, no divorce and no marriage—at least not in the sense of a legal contract. Marriage is, in Engels's terms, a matter of simple inclination and 'true sexual love'. Hence the title of this chapter.

Love, however, is the cause of what sadness and conflict exist in this society. In a famous passage Hammond outlines the emotional problems that still ruffle the utopian tranquillity, and how they are handled:

> We do not deceive ourselves, indeed, or believe that we can get rid of all the trouble that besets the dealings between the sexes. We know that we must face the unhappiness that comes of man and woman confusing the relations between natural passion, and sentiment, and the friendship which, when things go well, softens the awakening from passing illusions; but we are not so mad as to pile up degradation on that unhappiness by engaging in sordid squabbles about livelihood and position, and the power of tyrannising over the children who have been the result of love or lust.

He offers some examples of sexual trouble:

> Calf-love, mistaken for a heroism that shall be lifelong, yet early waning into disappointment; the inexplicable desire that comes on a man of riper years to be the all-in-all to some one woman, whose ordinary human kindness and human beauty he has idealised into superhuman perfection . . . ; or lastly the reasonable longing of a strong and thoughtful man to become the most intimate friend of some beautiful and wise woman . . . —as we exult

in all the pleasure and exaltation of spirit which goes with these things, so we set ourselves to bear the sorrow which not unseldom goes with them also.[18]

The treatment, if not the cure, is the kind of stoical response that Morris endeavoured to practise in his own emotional life; as he wrote in relation to his wife's intimacy with another man, 'how I long to keep the world from narrowing on me, and to look at things bigly and kindly!'[19] In Hammond's words:

> it is a point of honour with us not to be self-centred; not to suppose that the world must cease because one man is sorry; therefore, we should think it foolish, or if you will, criminal, to exaggerate these matters of sentiment and sensibility: we are no more inclined to eke out our emotional sorrows than to cherish our bodily pains: and we recognise that there are other pleasures besides love-making. You must remember also that we are long-lived, and that therefore beauty both in man and woman is not so fleeting as it was. . . . So we shake off these griefs in a way which perhaps the sentimentalists of other times would think contemptible and unheroic, but which we think necessary and manlike.[20]

We will return to this gendered language, first noting that Nowhere is essentially, though not rigidly, a monogamous society. Clara has lived with another man without censure before returning to Dick, but does not continue the relationships simultaneously or promiscuously. Later on, Ellen is partly in flight from more suitors than she can handle. When Guest asks about phalangsteries—what would today be called 'communes'—Hammond claims that such early socialist experiments in group living arose from poverty. In Nowhere, 'we like to live as a rule with certain house-mates that we have got used to', and separate dwellings are usual, although no door is shut to any good-tempered person who wants to join. But if household structures are flexible, there is no hint of sexual sharing, just as there is no suggestion of anything but heterosexual relationships beyond natural friendliness: utopian love is resolutely traditional in this respect. It is true that there is no outright condemnation or prohibition of gay or lesbian love, but in a work of fiction what is not mentioned does not and cannot exist. In Nowhere, heterosexuality rules.

It is interesting however that, given the virtual perfection of economic, social and environmental arrangements in Nowhere, 'love matters' provide the only arena for conflict. In the absence of competition over property and of compulsion to labour (Morris's view of work not being an orthodox Marxian one), there are few other areas in which quarrels arise. Although rare, murders occasionally happen as the result of hot temper and sudden violence, but the only instance described—as related by Walter Allen at Reading—is that of a rejected lover who attacks his rival with an axe and is accidentally killed in self-defence. The killer—who cannot really be called a murderer—is so stricken with remorse that he is liable to commit suicide, which makes the community very unhappy; indeed, the excitement and jealousy surrounding the tragedy make for an 'evil and feverish' atmosphere that must be dispelled. The solution is to isolate the 'criminal' and trust to the healing power of his love for the girl in question.

Unlike the examples cited by Hammond, both this tale and that of Clara's desertion of, and reunion with Dick, present love problems in terms of men rather than women as victims of rejection. In the utopian absence of all economic dependency and childcare difficulties, there is no reason to feel that women would be more vulnerable or disadvantaged if the roles were reversed, but the slant of the stories is significant. Just as emotional stoicism is heroic and 'manlike', so the ability to bewitch, or drive a man to violence, is a female attribute.

In this respect, the story follows the traditional contours of romance. In the real world of the 19th century, male desertion was the greater problem, among the proletariat as well as bourgeoisie, since social circumstances made women economically and emotionally vulnerable; in all classes, unsupported wives and mothers faced severe problems. And the function of romance fiction, in capitalist culture, is to obscure the facts of male power by proposing an emotional fantasy in which, finally, the right man surrenders his heart to a woman's power.

In *News from Nowhere*, women are implicitly given this sexual power over men. In a situation of absolute gender equality, such power might be mutual, for in a rational utopia there would, surely, be no unrequited love, even allowing for changes of partner. All would recognize the folly of unreciprocated desire and of demanding exclusive affection; love confers no rights and stakes no claims.

IV

Are romantic love, motherhood and happy housekeeping all that *News from Nowhere* has to offer women? If this is so, we would be justified in consigning it to the historical bin, recognizing it as a product of its patriarchal age and author, despite his otherwise progressive attitudes.

But although reactionary gender relations do form the bedrock of Morris's desirable society, it is also true that, as the story is told, the social and personal relations of men and women are rather more flexible and varied than this implies.

For one thing, the female characters are lively, acute and generally wiser than the men, and in the second part of the book, during the journey up the Thames, they feature more largely: Clara joins Dick as Guest's escort, and Ellen, who with her strange wild beauty can only be described as the heroine, takes over the central role of utopian interlocutor and guide.

On the way upriver, the social division of labour remains more or less traditional—the men do most of the rowing, and the women's participation in haymaking, although an example of shared labour, is presented more as festival than as everyday work. The masons dubbed obstinate refusers because they prefer building to haymaking are mainly male: half a dozen men and two women—Philippa and her daughter Kate. Now Philippa (inspired, it is said, by the success of Philippa Fawcett in attaining the highest marks in the mathematics final exams at Cambridge University) is the 'best carver', and accorded high status; but the masons' team-leader or foreman is a man.

It cannot be argued that, as in Bebel's prediction of life under socialism, the women in Nowhere all have equal opportunity and are not prevented from choosing 'masculine' pursuits, as Philippa appears to demonstrate. For in general the women spend their time in typically feminine affairs; Philippa is simply the exception that proves the rule. And beyond their housekeeping duties, they lead lives of what can only be termed idleness or, more politely, permanent holiday. Just as the weather is always fine, so the ladies are always leisured.

Now *News from Nowhere* is subtitled *An Epoch of Rest*, and central to its imagination is the freedom from the competitive struggle against poverty in arduous, insecure employment such as characterized much late 19th century labour in Britain. Morris knew himself to be an exception, even among his own class, in both freely choosing and enjoying his work, and his image of paradise is one where this freedom is extended to all. And there is no doubt that being freed from drudgery at home and at work would in large measure have greatly benefited working class women—those employed in laundries, sweatshops, manufacturing and domestic service—the main categories of female labour at this date. It would also have enhanced the lives of many in the lower reaches of the bourgeoisie.

The problem, from a feminist reader's perspective, now or then, is that however desirable the universal abolition of uncongenial work, this forms only part of the subjection of women. The social oppression of women has also to do with exclusion, with denial, with consciousness, definitions of difference and chauvinistic ideas about protection and special talents—that is, with all the sexist ideological impedimenta that accompanies and is invoked to justify economic oppression. It is all very well for there to be no jobs in Nowhere for lawyers or army commanders, for example—and we can all agree that in an ideal state these are unnecessary—when women have never had the opportunity to select or reject such work.

Equality and freedom for women as for other oppressed groups is a process of struggle and achievement—not secured on an individual or exceptional basis but as a general condition, without distinction of gender, class, skin colour or any of the other markers the rich and powerful use to exclude others. And one of the attractive aspects of *News from Nowhere* is indeed that its utopia is not simply represented as a given, magical state, but as something that has been fought for, gained and improved through conflict and argument. In its history, however, the gender issues of this struggle are subsumed in those of the class struggle, and thereby, as so often, ignored or evaded. Which would not matter too much—many details of the new Jerusalem are inevitably omitted from the tale—were it not for the fact that the position of women in the future so closely resembles that of women in the past, and that this was and is one of the specific items on the socialist agenda.

Even with Ellen this pattern is only slightly disturbed. She joins the travellers at Wallingford, rowing by herself—which was a more arresting image of independence in 1890 than it appears today—and shares the remainder of the sculling with Guest. Acute, affectionate and perceptive, she is the most ideal representative of the new society. Of all the persons 'in that world renewed', says Guest, 'she was the most unfamiliar to me, the most unlike what I could have thought of.' Clara, in comparison, reminds him of a very pleasant and unaffected young woman of his own time, whereas Ellen

> was not only beautiful with a beauty quite different from that of a 'young lady', but was in all ways so strangely interesting; so that I kept wondering what she would say or do next to surprise and please me. Not, indeed, that there was anything startling in what she actually said or did; but it was all done in a new way, and always with that indefinable interest and pleasure of life which I had noticed more or less in everybody, but which in her was more marked and more charming than in any one else that I had seen.[21]

She has knowledge, intelligence, ability, sensitivity and intuitive awareness beyond the reach of her compatriots. But these qualities are firmly linked to her femininity: she seems, to us, a perfect example of the sort of pretty woman by whom Guest would enjoy being ordered about, as one of 'the pleasantest forms of flirtation'.

V

News from Nowhere is therefore, undeniably and regrettably, a masculine vision of paradise. Furthermore, this is not simply a matter of its political statements, omissions and elisions. It is also as a literary text deeply imbued with the feeling and language of male desire. To a quite surprising degree, given the political origins of the book, this erotic thread is prominent throughout, from the first encounter with the blushing Annie through to Guest's final sorrow at losing Ellen. And the problematic nature of his lust is made explicit in the early morning at Runnymede when the three travellers glimpse Ellen in the garden; Guest protests at being left out of the fable Dick invents for the occasion and is told that he may imagine he is wearing the cap of darkness, seeing everything, himself invisible.

Guest responds sexually to all the women he meets, sometimes suspecting that they fancy Dick more than himself, and for various reasons is disappointed each time—the women vanish, or have lovers already. The disappointments pave the way for the meeting with Ellen, who has light hair and grey eyes, suntanned face and hands. When first seen she is lying on a sheepskin rug, and both her brown skin and bare feet are explicitly admired. The most openly erotic passage in the story is spoken by Dick, promising that Clara will look like Ellen after a summer spent haymaking:

> '. . . and we will manage to send you to bed pretty tired every night; and you will look so beautiful with your neck all brown, and your hands too, and you under your gown as white as privet . . .' The girl reddened very prettily and not for shame but pleasure . . .[22]

Guest's relationship with Ellen follows a courtship pattern. She leads—often literally taking him by the hand—with hints and promises of consummation:

> 'I should like to go with you all through the west country—thinking of nothing', concluded she, smiling.
> 'I should have plenty to think of', said I.[23]

and

> 'This evening, or tomorrow morning I shall make a proposal to you to do something which would please me very much, and I think would not hurt you. . . .'
> I broke in eagerly, saying that I would do anything in the world for her . . .[24]

Despite, or indeed because of, his frequent disparagement of his fifty-six years, it is clear that Guest's youthful lust has returned—such rejuvenation is a chief feature of this new life—and his slow, dreamy conversations with Ellen follow the movements of lovemaking, enacting the caresses and hesitations of sexual pleasure in syntax and language, most evidently in Chapter XXIX, describing the picnic lunch on the upper reaches of the Thames (too long to quote in full) which ends:

> As we went slowly down towards the boats she said again: 'Not for myself alone, dear friend; I shall have children; perhaps before the end a good many;—I hope so. And though of course I cannot force any special kind of knowledge upon them, yet, my friend, I cannot help thinking that just as they might be like me in body, so I might impress upon them some part of my ways of thinking; that is, indeed, some of the essential part of myself; that part which was not mere moods, created by the matters and events around me. What do you think?'
>
> Of one thing I was sure, that her beauty and kindness and eagerness combined, forced me to think as she did, when she was not earnestly laying herself open to receive my thoughts. I said, what at the time was true, that it was most important; and presently stood entranced by the wonder of her grace as she stepped into the light boat, and held out her hand to me. And so on we went up the Thames still—or whither?[25]

As a changeling, Guest cannot of course mate with an inhabitant of fairyland, so their intercourse—as Ellen 'lays herself open to receive my thoughts'—is that of philosophical discussion, and their children remain hypothetical, dream progeny. And their embraces are similarly displaced. 'On we went', says Guest, noting his 'new-born excitement about Ellen and my gathering fear of where it would land me', to arrive at their journey's end. Here Ellen makes her promised proposal, which is indeed no more than a chaste but meaningful invitation 'to live with us where we are going', and together they approach the old house. 'Take me on to the house at once', she whispers; 'we need not wait for the others; I had rather not.'

On the path, she gives a sensuous sigh of joy, as the climax is reached:

> She led me close to the house, and laid her shapely sun-browned hand and arm on the lichened wall as if to embrace it, and cried out 'Oh me! O me! How I love the earth, and the seasons, and weather, and all things that deal with it, and all that grows out of it—as this has done!'
> I could not answer her or say a word. Her exultation and pleasure were so keen and exquisite, and her beauty, so delicate yet so interfused with energy, expressed it so fully, that any added word would have been commonplace and futile. I dreaded lest the others should come in suddenly and break the spell she had cast about me; but we stood there a while by the corner of the big gable of the house, and no one came. . . .[26]

Yet of course, there is no happy ending to this romance. As in an erotic dream, the narrator must wake before fulfilment, at the village feast in the church, when he stands on the threshold with an expectant smile, ready for the festivity. Suddenly, the vision begins to slip; he becomes invisible and turns to Ellen, whose face saddens:

> she shook her head with a mournful look, and the next moment all consciousness of my presence had faded from her face.[27]

VI

The fact that the loss of paradise takes place at the feast, in a social setting, however, indicates that sexual love or desire is only part of the vision of the future, although the erotic suffuses the depiction of Nowhere. Lust (in its original root-sense of passion rather than vice) in fact works, throughout the text, as metaphor or carriage for utopian desire, just as Ellen stands, in her strange wild beauty, as a personification of the new age, at once alluring and unattainable.

For it is longing that drives *News from Nowhere*, from the opening cry of the narrator 'If I could but see a day of it! If I could but see it!' And it is the sense of impossibility that sustains the reader's answering desire—for, once attained, satisfaction or joy begin to dwindle: utter happiness is always out of reach, or fades into banality, giving rise to discontent. And it is Morris's skill in holding this emotional yearning dramatically in tension with the social perfection of Nowhere that takes his narrative beyond the notion of a blueprint, with every detail 'correctly' sketched in.

In his discussion of socialist utopias, E. P. Thompson (quoting from Miguel Abensour, and without specifically mentioning the erotic thrust of *News from Nowhere*) noted that what distinguishes Morris's enterprise 'is, exactly, its open, speculative quality, and its detachment of the imagination from the demands of conceptual precision'. More important than whether you approve or disapprove of its formulations regarding utopian economics, or gender relations, or whatever, 'is the challenge to the imagination to become immersed in the same open exploration':

> in such an adventure two things happen: our habitual values (the 'commonsense' of bourgeois society) are thrown into disarray. And we enter into Utopia's proper and new-found space: *the education of desire* . . . 'to teach desire to desire, to desire better, to desire more, and above all to desire in a different way'.[28] [original italics]

After talking of past miseries with Guest, Clara senses unhappiness in the air, 'as if we were longing for something that we cannot have'. As she also suggests, one problem with utopia is complacency and shallowness, since life leaves nothing to be desired. Happiness, indeed, can only be known by contrast with its lack. Again, Morris skilfully succeeds in endowing his utopia with this consciousness, which saves it from smugness. And it is, I think, an index of the passionate strength of Morris's socialist desire that eroticism, finally subordinated to social fellowship, so frankly shapes the feeling and language of *News from Nowhere*, not as an intellectual exercise but as an expression of the plainest human need and demand for joy. Without such desire, there can be no hope. And in the final analysis what matters, and makes the text continually worth re-reading and re-printing, is not so much the unsatisfactory images of women's position in the supposedly free and equal society of the 21st century, but the immediate challenge to our own imaginations to desire more, and better, and in a different way, in order to change things.

₰ 6 ₰

An Old House Amongst New Folk:
Making Nowhere Somewhere

COLIN WARD

I NEVER EXPECTED TO FIND MYSELF at a party in a 20th-storey penthouse on the Duquesne Heights at the point where the Allegheny and Monongahela rivers join to become the mighty Ohio. I turned my back on the spectacle of Pittsburg's Golden Triangle on Light-Up Night because a fellow guest was a twinkling-eyed, white-bearded 81-year-old, Carl Feiss, former professor of architecture at Columbia University.

He had been the assistant to the architect Raymond Unwin (1863–1940), when Unwin became Director of the Planning and Housing Division there in 1936. And when Unwin lay dying in Connecticut in 1940 he gave to Feiss various bits of 'beloved trivia' as mementoes. There was the ivory pocket rule and the small pair of dividers Unwin always carried in his pocket to measure scales on plans, and there was the little vellum-bound copy of *News from Nowhere* that Unwin took around with him and which he inscribed to Carl Feiss, who told me how Unwin stressed that this book was the key to every one of his architectural, social and political opinions.[1]

In practice, of course, Unwin was like the rest of us, a disillusioned utopian who had accepted every kind of compromise with the world as it is, just to get something done here and now. As early as 1902 he had exclaimed '. . . How we loved our Morris when he came to us sharing our illusions, full of life and joy . . . ,'[2] and thirty years later, paying tribute to another of Morris's architectural disciples, William Richard Lethaby (1867–1931), he returned to this theme of *joy*:

At the Lethaby evening at the RIBA in 1932 Unwin returned to the belief underlying 'the joy which Lethaby and William Morris took in Gothic art: that is, their belief that it gave great opportunities for enjoyment to the workman . . .' and affirmed 'I still retain the conviction that some day we shall again find a style of building which will afford an opportunity for joy to all the workmen who are engaged on it', although he admitted that 'we do not seem to be approaching much nearer at the present time'.[3]

Unwin's early writings, both before and after the publication of *News from Nowhere*, with their advocacy of the collegiate plan of buildings around a quadrangle and of communally prepared and served meals in a common dining room and kitchen, have an almost uncanny resemblance to the architectural landscape that Morris described. For example, writing in June 1889 in *The Commonweal*, the journal in which Morris was to serialize *News from Nowhere* in the following year, Unwin describes the Sunday outing of the Chesterfield socialists to an early 18th-century house, Sutton Hall, in words that sound as though they had slipped out of Morris's text:

> Small wonder that, as we stood looking at the house and the splendid view it commands, we should fall to talking of the 'days that are going to be', when this Hall and others like it will be the centre of a happy communal life. Plenty of room in that large house for quite a small colony to live, each one having his own den upstairs . . . and downstairs would be large common dining-halls, smoking rooms—if indeed life shall still need the weed to make it perfect.
>
> And we chatted on, each adding a bit to our picture; how some would till the land around and others tend the cattle, while others perhaps would start some industry, working in the outbuildings or building workshops in the park, and taking care not to spoil our view . . .'[4]

Unwin went on to become the designer and planner of New Earswick, outside York, of Letchworth, the first of the two Garden Cities developed by another utopian, Ebenezer Howard (who believed that Morris, like Ruskin, Kropotkin and others, had only failed 'by a hair's breadth' to develop their own garden cities,[5]) and then of the Hampstead Garden Suburb. On a balmy summer day in any of these quiet domestic environments it is easy to imagine that we have wandered into the landscape of *News from Nowhere*.

Indeed the particular characteristics of Morris's book that lift it above 'the dullness and artificiality' that our best historian of utopian travels, Marie Louise Berneri, found to be typical of most utopian writers of the period, rest on three things. The first is that Morris is a libertarian, and does not turn his personal preferences into rules for the whole of humankind. The second is that 'the persuasive charm of *News from Nowhere* does not reside so much in the admittedly convincing arguments put forward by its various utopian inhabitants to explain why they have chosen their manner of life, but in the atmosphere of beauty, freedom, calm and happiness which pervades the whole story.'[6] The third is that Morris, with his passionate feeling for architecture and its setting, permanently affects the way sympathetic readers view reality.

There is a passage in the book where Morris describes his traveller's arrival at the house which is evidently Kelmscott:

> We crossed the road, and again almost without my will my hand raised the latch of a door in the wall, and we stood presently on a stone path which led up to the old house. . . . My companion gave a sign of pleased surprise and enjoyment; nor did I wonder, for the garden between the wall and the house was redolent of the June flowers, and the roses were rolling over one another with that delicious super-abundance of small well-tended gardens which at first sight takes away all thought from the beholder save that of beauty. The blackbirds were singing their loudest, the doves were cooing on the roof-ridge, the rooks in the high elm-trees beyond were garrulous among the young leaves, and the swifts wheeled whining about the gables. And the house itself was a fit guardian for all the beauty of this heart of summer.[7]

The scene formed the frontispiece for the Kelmscott edition of Morris's book. I felt the same sensation in a different climate when I paid a visit to Melsetter House, built by one of Morris's architectural disciples, Lethaby, on the island of Hoy in Orkney. A walled garden was a necessity there because of the high winds and after I had walked through it the then 90-year-old owner allowed me to wander through the rooms, with their original furnishings from Morris and Company, and I really felt, on that bleak northern island, as though I had stepped into the pages of Morris's romance.

Readers of the volume of the letters exchanged between Frederic Osborn and Lewis Mumford will recall that Mumford felt an identical sensation, not in Utopia but in Welwyn Garden City. He told Osborn that 'the breakfasts in your garden have almost indissolubly mingled in my mind with the kind of morning fragrance that William Morris put into the opening pages of *News from Nowhere,* so that I feel that I have actually had a foot in utopia at one moment in my life; a feeling that I never had as a mere visitor anywhere else before . . . '[8]

It would be an intriguing experiment in enviromental psychology and in the techniques of architectural appraisal to filter out the qualities that give any particular group of buildings a high NNQ (*News from Nowhere* quotient). I don't believe that it is in the slightest degree a matter of architectural style. After all, Morris's account of the arrival at Kelmscott was written in terms of birds and gardens, not of the building. And after all, Osborn's house in Welwyn was not an arts-and-crafts building at all, it was a sub-Georgian house designed by Louis de Soissons in a style that Morris deprecated, though he would have approved the choice of materials. There are buildings of all periods which have a high NNQ, often they are very ordinary houses in ordinary places, quite often they are slung-together shacks built by the merest *bricoleur,* and sometimes they are the work of modern movement architects.

Let us try to identify the NNQ factors. The one that was most passionately held by Morris himself, was that of joy in the work of building. The passages from the writings of Raymond Unwin that I have quoted on this theme are drawn from Mark Swenarton's elegant study of the evolution of this idea which he sees as originating with the work of John Ruskin. By the time, in 1853, that Ruskin came to write the third volume of *The Stones of Venice,* he concluded that the secret of the glory of Gothic building was that the workman was free to find pleasure and creativity in the work.

When Morris at the Kelmscott Press reprinted Ruskin's chapter called 'On the Nature of Gothic, and the Office of the Workman therein', in 1892, he wrote a preface in which he made the impressive statement that this chapter 'in future days will be considered one of the very few necessary and inevitable utterances of the century'.[9]

Swenarton carefully traces this belief through Morris's work and through that of Philip Webb (1831–1915), who tried hard but failed to integrate his architecture with his emerging socialism; that of W.R. Lethaby, who was inspired by it in the founding of the Central School of Arts and Crafts and of the Brixton School of Building; that of Raymond Unwin, and that of Arthur J. Penty (1875–1937), who inspired the Building Guilds of the early 1920s (who later succumbed to the ideology of Mussolini's corporate state). He even teases out Ruskin's influence on Frank Lloyd Wright, Le Corbusier and Walter Gropius. For the work of the first generation of Arts and Crafts architects had inspired a monumental 3-volume book *Das Englische Haus* in which Hermann Muthesius summed up Ruskin's message:

> Ruskin was the first to reach the point of calling in to question machine civilization as a whole. He maintained that it made man himself a machine since it forced him to spend his whole life performing a single mechanical operation and was thus literally death to the worker's spiritual and material wellbeing.[10]

Like the rest of us, Swenarton has no difficulty in pointing to the fallacies of the Ruskinian approach and to the likelihood that few of Ruskin's disciples had ever actually been on a building site and that fewer still were acquainted with building workers, and 'were therefore able to indulge in fantasies about the supposed pleasures of labour and the supposed attributes of the labourer'.[11] Correct, no doubt, but Philip Webb, for example, would always act as general contractor himself and would engage individual tradesmen personally, and I myself have seen an elderly Arts and Crafts architect explaining to a bricklayer on site how he would have a better time and produce a better building if he increased the lime content and reduced the cement content of the mortar. Morris's disciples, in building just as in furniture-making, kept alive old practices which had been lost in the industries themselves. This is why so many, like Morris himself, abandoned the profession of architecture to become craftsmen themselves.

The second of these NNQ factors relates to something Morris took completely for granted: the fact that traditional building materials grow old gracefully. Stone, timber, brick, clay and straw may wear out, they may erode and split and leak. They may become impractical for the building user, but when properly maintained, they last better than the materials of building a century later. Even in decline, they are not offensive. The architectural landscape of *News from Nowhere*, and indeed of all his writings, is one of building materials which improve by ageing and by loving care and selective renewal. A century later structural components he deplored, like cast iron or even corrugated iron, have acquired their own patina of pleasing decay in the form of oxidization, moss and lichens. Morris, who, knowing the horrors of restoration, favoured leaving old buildings alone, would have been flummoxed by our own dilemmas. But he would point to the elementary fact that most of the building materials we use today deteriorate from the moment they are on the site, while the components of the built environment of *News from Nowhere* improve in appearance from the moment that, fresh, raw and new, they are put in place, so that in a few years they will mellow to become an inevitable and cherished part of the environment.

This raises the third NNQ factor. Morris's work, in and out of *News from Nowhere* assumes something that he took for granted: the mutual accommodation of the human and the natural world. At an elementary level, the worst of buildings becomes 'humanized' as we quaintly put it, by the fact that plants will grow up it or around it, trees and bushes will screen it, but also provide something for the occupants to watch, changing throughout the seasons, out of the window. At a communal level, Morris can be seen as a precursor of not only the Garden City movement, but of the whole 20th century exodus from the grotesquely overcrowded industrial city of his own day.

Morris wanted, in the passages selected by Paul Thompson, 'neither the towns to be appendages of the country, nor the country of the town: I want the town to be impregnated with the beauty of the country, and the country with the intelligence and vivid life of the town. I want every homestead to be clean, orderly and tidy; a lovely house surrounded by acres and acres of garden. On the other hand, I want the town to be clean, orderly and tidy; in short, a garden with beautiful houses in it.'[12] He similarly thought that 'Every child should be able to play in a garden close to the place where his parents live',[13] and to this end, seeking a balance between town and country, 'I even demand that there be left waste places and wilds in it.'

All Morris's hopes and fears in the area that we now call town and country planning, as well as his aspirations for a simple, vernacular architecture, are put into an imaginative context in *News from Nowhere*. The actual preferences of that proportion of his fellow citizens a century later who have been able to choose their own environment, indicate that most people agree with him. Making this choice available to all is a political issue, just as Morris always insisted that it was.

Study the preferred domestic environments of the 1990s, as displayed in the 'neo-vernacular' estates of speculative builders, or the prices paid for converted barns and granaries, or the out-of-town hypermarkets designed like farm-yards with acres of hand-made clay tiles on their steeply-pitched roofs, the make-believe ruralism, the magazines devoted to selling the paraphernalia of 'country living', and you see a kind of parody of Morris's vision. The visual trimmings, but not the substance.

But in the architectural world there has always been a handful of architects consciously working in the tradition inspired by Morris. Their work was seldom published, their commissions were few, they tended to be one-person practices, giving a direct, personal and professional service to their clients. They keep getting re-discovered when a perceptive visitor stumbles across a building that grows old gracefully, that merges into the landscape, but is distinguished by the quality of detailing and the signs of loving care devoted to modest simple structures. The generation actually trained in the Arts-and-Crafts tradition has died out, but has been continually replaced by new recruits whose attributes would be seen by Morris as those of fellow-workers, even though their architectural idiom was far from his.

This claim can be made for contemporary architects like Ralph Erskine, or Giancarlo de Carlo, and most certainly for David Lea who declares that:

An architecture which expresses a planetary vision, rather than an abstract technological romanticism, would be, as in the Middle Ages, rooted in its own region. Though it is impossible to achieve with any degree of purity in these days, we can work towards it if we look for the non-technological solution at the planning stage, use low energy materials, include the material's life in assessment of building costs, start from traditional techniques, simplify and purify construction details; plan to trap heat and sunlight, and avoid complicated mechanical systems; cut down hours of alienating paper work, and help building users to take back control of the building process and the planning and design of their villages and neighbourhoods.[14]

To my mind the contemporary architect who most completely epitomized Morris's approach a century later was Walter Segal (1907–1985), and this is a judgement loaded with paradox. For Segal was an architect totally wedded to the Modern Movement, always seeking appropriate uses for new synthetic materials. He was reared in an anarchist commune in the Ticino canton of Switzerland, trained as an architect in Germany, absorbed the message of Philip Webb and W.R. Lethaby through the book by Muthesius and actually met Raymond Unwin when he was obliged to emigrate to England.

Segal did not shirk the biggest challenge of the Morris-Ruskin tradition on the nature of work and the status of the worker, and he tried to re-express it in a way that was shorn of romanticism:

> He was, however, deeply concerned about the traditionally anti-social and hazardous nature of the building industry and this helped form his own method of construction. 'I am thinking about the need to improve the working conditions in the industry which will allow it to attract more capable men and women. We offer in the building industry some of the worst working conditions that exist.' He was equally scathing of the nostalgia for outdated craftsmanship and glorification of 'honest toil' which he felt had trickled right through to Gropius from William Morris. 'Would Morris have liked the look of a Black and Decker drill?' he asked, 'I fear not.' All Segal's activity has implicitly followed that motto which is, however, attributed to Morris: 'I

want to design things that people get pleasure in making, and to make things that people get pleasure in using.'

Over the gable of a fine old timber house in the Bernese Oberland, 200 years old, are written the words: *Master K and his men did everything to my entire satisfaction.* 'Please note', added Walter Segal, 'not merely to his *reasonable* satisfaction as stipulated in the RIBA Contract. On how many houses in post-war England could this be written?'[15]

In this passage Segal's biographer John McKean bridges the gap between the alleged unreality of Morris's views on work and the actual situation of the building worker in contemporary Britain. He is raising an issue of immense importance for those of Morris's readers for whom his book is something more than a contribution to ruralist make-believe.

Segal himself developed a system of timber-framed house-building, with links, as he always claimed, with the American method of 'balloon-frame' construction, and with medieval frame construction as well as with the Japanese tradition of building. Late in his life he experienced a demand from private clients for houses built in his method as it was cheap and simple. A carpenter, Mr Wade, would follow him around from job to job, but slowly it became apparent that the clients could do more and more of the work for themselves. Segal fretted over the issue of making this method available to all. Why couldn't families on local authority waiting lists build their own houses? Eventually it happened, in the London Borough of Lewisham.[16] The result was a triumph. One of the self-builders, Ken Atkins, said, 'The house took me and the wife eleven months to build. It is an adaptable building, unusual yes, but extremely nice to live in. The sheer joy of putting a spade in the ground ... well it's an indescribable feeling . . . you finally have control over what you are doing in your life.'[17]

For Segal himself it was the vindication of the hopes of a lifetime: 'What I found astonishing with these people,' he said, 'was the direct personal friendly contact that I had with them and which they had among themselves. And quite beyond that the tapping of their own ideas—countless small variations and innovations, and additions were made by them. . . . But it is astonishing that there is among the people that live in this country such a wealth of talent.'[18] The moral world of *News from Nowhere* had actually been brought to life in a London borough.

I am convinced that Morris would have recognized, beyond architectural incompatibilities and disappointed hopes, that his spirit is alive and well a century later.

❧ 7 ❧

The Hammersmith Guest House again:
William Morris and the Architecture of Nowhere

MARK PEARSON

VISITORS TO THE MASSIVE TITHE BARN at Great Coxwell in Oxfordshire have occasionally entered to discover prostrate figures in the centre of the building gazing sternly up into the roof timbers. They are not injured, they are students of architecture, for it has long been held that the view from this supine position yields an immediate grounding in the practical arts of structure and construction of buildings. Yet very few of them will know of Morris's great admiration for this agrarian 'cathedral', nor of the vital repairs to save it made by the society which he founded, the SPAB.[1] Morris considered it to be one of the finest buildings in England,[2] and it is surprising and unfortunate that William Guest was not allowed to stay long enough to encounter the barn at the end of his journey in *News from Nowhere*. Surely we have been denied a moving and lucid description of this great building seeming, as it does, to grow from the Earth. This is indeed ironic since it might well have provided us with a single simple statement of Morris's understanding of architecture. The coherent but fragmentary evidence we otherwise glean from the story is perhaps symptomatic of his lifelong relationship to the 'mother of the arts'—which was largely indirect. The general difficulty in establishing a critical position for Morris in relation to architecture is that his involvement with the subject has been continually interwoven with the work of Philip Webb. The proximity of the two men throughout their creative lives has meant that for architectural observers the more accessible work of Webb, the practitioner, has too often been taken as a direct paradigm for the thoughts of Morris, who, uniquely in this subject, was merely a theorist.[3] *News from Nowhere* provides us with a distinct and independent account of the form that the built environment might take as a consequence of his utopian vision.

In this chapter we shall attempt to assimilate this position and then draw a comparison with Webb's work at that time. The divergence of thought that we shall identify will suggest that *News from Nowhere* might simultaneously represent a potential beginning and an end for architecture at the eve of the twentieth century.

Before leaving our students, recumbent in the barn, we might wonder how, if not by Morris, they came to know of the building and its qualities? The answer almost certainly lies in the lineage, identified initially by Nikolaus Pevsner, from William Morris to Walter Gropius and beyond.[4] This second and popular coupling between Morris and the architectural theories of the modern movement is again misleading, since we shall see that it is true only in part. It was an historical chain based largely upon design seen as an autonomous activity and not, as Morris would have insisted, within a broader social context. It has at least ensured that Great Coxwell has still some influence upon the collective consciousness of twentieth century architects even if the barn's most important admirer and the reasons for his applause are now forgotten.

Our first encounter with new architecture in the novel is not in the form of a building, but with a bridge:

> I had perhaps dreamed of such a bridge, but never seen such an one out of an illuminated manuscript; for not even the Ponte Vecchio at Florence came anywhere near it. It was of stone arches, splendidly solid and as graceful as they were strong; high enough also to let ordinary river traffic through easily. Over the parapet showed quaint and fanciful little buildings, which I supposed to be booths or shops, beset with painted and guilded vanes and spirelets. The stone was a little weathered, but showed no marks of the grimey sootiness which I was used to on every London building more than a year old. In short, to me a wonder of a bridge.[5]

This new stone structure had been constructed to replace the suspension bridge at Hammersmith which Morris refers to in an earlier passage as 'ugly'. When we examine the qualities which are applauded in the description we begin to understand that issues such as permanence, usage, performance and cleanliness are unfamiliar factors which for Morris influence its 'beauty'. In contrast to the cold and windy suspension structure it appears to support social activity and occupation. It is therefore a bridge that connects rather than divides the communities on either side. But the reference to the Ponte Vecchio is perplexing, since although in appearance the Italian Gothic might nearly represent the aesthetic qualities desired by Morris, the high density of occupation in central Florence which has provoked the urban 'colonization' of that bridge seems absent in the revived Hammersmith:

> Both shores had a line of very pretty houses, low and not large, standing back a little from the river . . . There was a continuous garden in front of them . . . Behind the houses I could see great trees rising, mostly planes, and looking down the water there were the reaches towards Putney almost as if they were a lake with a forest shore.[6]

In contrast the Ponte Vecchio connects the banks of the Arno which has four and five storey buildings forming cliffs tight against the river on either side. Whilst Ray Watkinson is undoubtedly correct in his statement, ' . . . his thoughts about building are always his thoughts about living relations',[7] it is quite often the poetic and not the prosaic aspects of these relations which, for Morris, generates the architecture. Therefore, the link between the social and architectural structures in News from Nowhere is not simply causal and pragmatic—but motivated. The buildings described are not merely products of the new epoch, they embody its 'spirit'. John Hanna, in his excellent lecture 'The Politics of Architecture', makes interesting comparisons between Morris and the French 20th century architect Le Corbusier.[8] Whilst there are clear parallels in much of their thought, a fundamental difference arises in their perception of the relationship between architecture and society. In News from Nowhere the built environment has gradually evolved under the growing influence of the new social conditions. We learn from Old Hammond in the chapter 'How the Change Came' that the new society was established following a bloody, but necessary, revolution.

Only then did the architectural product begin to transform as craft skills were re-learnt and the new relationship between the people and the land emerged. Conversely, Le Corbusier's notion in 'Towards a New Architecture'[9] was that his new architecture, once established, would eventually promote a change in social attitudes, whilst in the meantime revolution would be avoided.[10] The two positions are clearly opposed in that Morris understands architecture to be the product of a given society, whilst Le Corbusier suggests that architecture might itself condition and in some way determine that society. In reality there is, of course, some truth in both notions, but the philosophical gulf which divides them, as proposals for the instrumental mechanics of Utopia, is immense. It has been to the chagrin of the built environment that the macho optimism of Le Corbusier's position has appeared seductive to so many twentieth century architects of much lesser ability (clearly if architecture is believed to generate its own sympathetic audience then it can hardly fail!). On one hand we have the centralized, state-led proposals of Le Corbusier whilst on the other there is the devolved society of Nowhere, generating an individual and localized architectural expression. Morris's concept neatly supports the idea of building seen as a folk-art, which is naturally a major theme of his descriptions in *News from Nowhere*.

In the novel, whilst architecture is still the 'mother of the arts' it does not appear to be anything more than the sum of its parts—its 'craft children'. The architectural valency of each building is seen simply as a direct manifestation of technique and materials. We can see therefore that Morris's position is, in this respect, clearly a fore-runner of the Modern Movement dictums of the early twentieth century[11]. But sadly, it would not be the techniques of craft production but those of the new 'machine age' which would fashion the architectural object in the next epoch. However, the essential postulate of a mono-semantic causality in design *was* developed from Morris, and it is in this sense that Pevsner is most profound in establishing him as his first 'pioneer' of modern design. This direct and systematic relationship between labour (craft technique) and artistic expression had also the effect of initiating the theme of 'morality' which would characterize architectural debate for so much of this century.[12]

Let us consider this proposition of an architectural expression developed solely from craft technique. The relationship between Morris, the theoretician, and Webb, the practitioner, may be understood as problematic in this context. The architectural designer is presumably subjugated to the status of craft co-ordinator and has only to design the framework within which the masons, carpenters, plasterers etc might operate.[13] Whilst we meet tradesmen at work, and hear descriptions of their products within the text, no mention is made of how the overall design of the buildings was arrived at. It seems probable that the new society has abolished the traditional role of architect as singular creator in favour of collective decision-making between the crafts people.

> You see, we all think this the prettiest place for a house, up and down these reaches; and the site has been so long encumbered with an unworthy one, that we masons were determined to pay off fate and destiny for once and build the prettiest house we could compass here . . .[14]

Whilst Morris's precedent for positing the master mason as architect is certainly the medieval building site, it is worthy to note that less structured societies of today still operate successfully on this basis. Bernard Rudofsky's seminal volume, *Architecture without Architects*[15] is still the best evidence that sophisticated and often very ordered solutions can be produced without recourse to a specialist designer. It would seem that this demise of the architect as a remote designer is the logical conclusion to, and an extension of, Ruskin's argument initiated in *The Nature of Gothic*:

> Understand this clearly: You can teach a man to draw a straight line, and to cut one; to strike a curved line, and to carve it; and to copy and to carve any number of lines or forms, with an admirable speed and perfect precision; and you find his work perfect of its kind: but if you ask him to think about any of those forms, to consider if he cannot find any better in his own head, he stops; his execution becomes hesitating; he thinks, and ten to one he thinks wrong; ten to one he makes a mistake in the first touch he gives to his work as a thinking being. But you have made a man of him for all that. He was only a machine before, an animated tool.[16]

Clearly the only satisfactory relationship between the designer and the maker, in Ruskin as in *News from Nowhere* is for them to be co-existent.

This was not the way in which Webb operated. Margaret Richardson makes a telling observation that his working drawings '. . . leave nothing to the builder. He knew everything about materials, and acted as the "upper foreman" on paper.' She quotes from a drawing:

> The carving to be / particularly done according to this design, keeping the curves / modelling, sections etc. as here indicated. It should be clearly / and freely cut so as to give effect to the design as intended and / expressed by the drawing—clean-cut and effective tool-marks / to be left at completion . . .[17]

There are two further Ruskinian influences upon the architecture encountered in the story by William Guest. The first develops from the new attitude to work and its consequent scarcity. This appears to give rise to the highly decorated façade of the building near Goring since its execution then requires longer, but pleasurable, toil. The head carver, Mistress Philippa, is warned about her over-enthusiasm for her work. 'Now Philippa, if you gobble up your work like that, you will soon have none to do; and what will become of you then?'[18] Philippa clearly demonstrates Morris's definition of art as 'pleasure in labour' but we learn that the form of the decoration also corresponds to principles which accord with Ruskin: '. . . we want to carve a kind of wreath of flowers and figures all round it'.[19] The floral design could therefore be taken direct from nature with the girl, Kate, as a life-model for the figure subjects.

Decoration on other buildings is more sparing and, earlier in the story, we are given a description of the guest house at Hammersmith in which William initially stays. It is a red-brick building with a lead roof, and external decoration is reduced to 'a frieze of figure subjects in baked clay, very well executed, and designed with a force and directness which I had never noticed in modern work before'.[20] Since the building was constructed in 1962, soon after the revolution, then presumably work was less scarce and the architectural style therefore more direct. John Hanna[21] has identified two distinct periods in the post-revolutionary era; these correspond to the separate languages represented by the two buildings above, which are those most clearly described in the story.

This reasonable justification for a varied and heterogeneous stock of building appears not to have been a post-rationalization of a picturesque aesthetic. We might also recall Thompson's observation that 'the choices before men in a Communist society (he saw) were numerous, the manifestations of their social life would take many forms'.[22] The idiosyncrasies of individuals would therefore be borne out in their dwelling places. We hear in the story of several types of house but perhaps the most ideologically significant is the communal dwelling house, although most people seem to live still in detached houses or cottages. In the main street of Hammersmith, William Guest observes,

> There were houses about, some on the road, some amongst the fields with pleasant lanes leading down to them, and each surrounded by a teeming garden. They were all pretty in design, and as solid as might be, but countryfied in appearance, like yeoman's dwellings; some of them red brick, like those by the river, but more of timber and plaster, which were by the necessity of their construction so like medieval houses of the same materials that I fairly felt as if I were alive in the fourteenth century.[23]

That crucial phrase, 'by the necessity of their construction' confirms Morris's belief that a return to craft-technique and traditional building methods together with the strengthened individualism in society would naturally produce the romantic and informal imagery of the picturesque. We see, clearly stated, the historicist behaviourism which Morris inherited from Ruskin and which was then shared with the Arts and Crafts Movement as a whole. The essential reference to the Middle Ages can be traced back to Pugin's 'Contrasts' of 1836 from which point on

> Medieval production was to become synonymous with 'natural' production, transforming the plea for medievalism into a sententious criticism of the 'un-naturalness' of mechanised industrial production.[24]

The greatest architectural praise is indeed reserved for a truly medieval building, Morris's country residence, Kelmscott Manor,

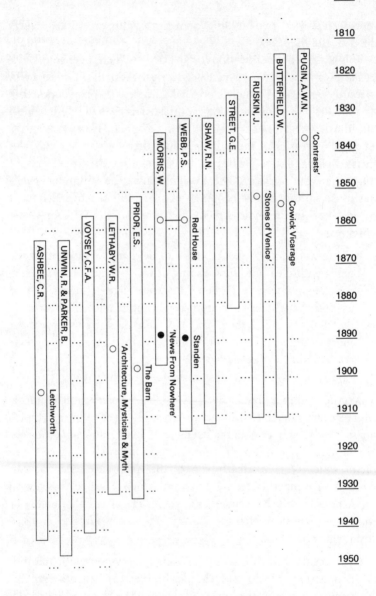

	1800
	1810
PUGIN, A.W.N.	1820
BUTTERFIELD, W.	
RUSKIN, J.	1830
STREET, G.E.	
SHAW, R.N.	'Contrasts'
WEBB, P.S.	1840
MORRIS, W.	1850
	Cowick Vicarage
PRIOR, E.S.	'Stones of Venice'
	Red House
LETHABY, W.R.	1860
VOYSEY, C.F.A.	1870
UNWIN, R. & PARKER, B.	1880
ASHBEE, C.R.	1890
	'News From Nowhere' Standen
	1900
	The Barn
	'Architecture, Mysticism & Myth'
	1910
	Letchworth
	1920
	1930
	1940
	1950

Figure 2: Progenitors and Architects of the Arts & Crafts
Movement—a simplified chronological chart.

which we discover as the destination of William Guest in his journey up the Thames. It is Ellen, his companion, who embraces the old building exclaiming 'O me! O me! How I love the earth, and the seasons, and weather, and all things that deal with it, and all that grows out of it,—as this has done!'[25] It is this empathy with the environment that Morris wishes to applaud in ancient buildings, and ultimately motivates his propositions with regard to new architecture, which we examined earlier. We can summarize this concern in terms of two complementary meta-narratives—'nature' and 'tradition'—which either together or independently justify each of his proposals, which are seen as 'natural', 'traditional' or both.

Webb's biographer, Lethaby, highlights the importance of tradition in an understanding of the environment (attributed to both Morris and Webb): 'The land was not merely "nature", it was the land which had been laboured over by the generations of men; buildings were not "architecture", they were builded history and poetry.'[26]

Figure 2 is a chronological chart which indicates some of the critical progenitors of the Arts and Crafts Movement together with six of its more important exponents from the next generation of practising architects. The chart illustrates that the years around 1890 were in fact vital to the development of the Movement. The work at this time of Webb and Shaw, who had both been pupils under the Gothic Revival architect Street, and the thoughts of Morris, were an essential link between the established texts of Ruskin and Pugin and the rising avant-garde, who were just embarking upon their careers in design.

The seminal success of Red House may be seen as an alliance of two separate sets of generative tactics. Espousing the principles of Ruskin and Pugin but employing a constructional syntax developed by Webb from Butterfield , the building's inspiration was a simultaneous response to ideas which were both theoretical and practical.

From this perfect synthesis, in 1859, Morris and Webb developed their methodologies independently, but in parallel. The influence which they each had upon the architecture of the Arts and Crafts Movement was therefore quite distinct even though their ideological arguments were essentially similar.

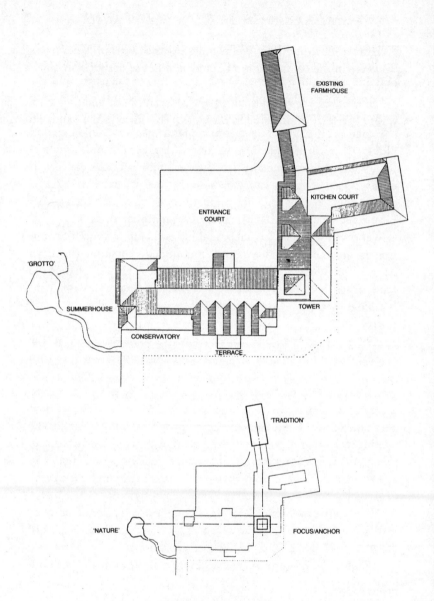

Figure 3: Standen, East Grinstead (Webb)—simplified roof plan and 'Ideogram'.

Figure 3 illustrates how Webb embodies the ideals of *News from Nowhere* in the composition of Standen, a house designed in 1891 near East Grinstead.

The Modern Movement cult of 'the plan', if not originating with Webb, is clearly anticipated in his work. This idea, in the hands of orthodox modernists, would eventually deny the typological approach which Morris appears to favour. Webb marshalls the accommodation at Standen to make manifest the symbolic programme whereas 'the plan' would become axiomatic to the Modern Movement as the means by which the functional programme might be organized and represented. In this way modern architecture lost the ability to represent anything other than merely what it was.[27]

A formal, rather than functional, typology would not fully reappear as a theoretical position until the work of the Italian Aldo Rossi in the 1970s. Rossi represents an interesting parallel to Morris, since although ideologically he shares a Marxist viewpoint his outlook is essentially pessimistic. Whereas *News from Nowhere* describes a coherent stable environment (the book's sub-title is 'An Epoch of Rest'), Rossi's 'Analagous City' is a fragmentary anti-utopia thriving on conflict and discontinuity. It is continuity which underwrites Morris's respect for typology and may have been the quality which made Kelmscott Manor so endearing.

When Standen was conceived, the idea of creating a motivated plannimetric composition which might provoke a particular 'reading' of the building was just emerging. The notion of type had certainly been expressed earlier in the nineteenth century. 'The art of building is born out of a pre-existing germ; nothing whatsoever comes from nothing.' Clearly ideas regarding 'type' are closely related to those concerning tradition and in particular its progressive role *vis-à-vis* the creative act, in which types might be seen 'not as image[s] of a thing to be copied or completely imitated, but as idea[s] which in themselves ought to serve as guiding rules.'[28]

E.P. Thompson[29] notes Morris's enthusiasm for Thomas More's *Utopia* (1516) and a comparison with the architectural descriptions of that proposed society has some distinct parallels with Nowhere. First, the population is dispersed evenly throughout the country (although gathered together in fifty-four towns of 80,000 people each).

Extensive gardens are a significant feature of the housing areas and larger communal buildings serve every thirty houses. The dwellings are not privately owned, but well built and continually maintained. Although they are comfortable, they are also basic and lacking in luxury. However, unlike Morris, More sees very little need for individuality to be expressed by the architecture. The three-storey, flat roofed houses are all similar and the towns are identical with regular planning and streets which are wide and straight. We see that although much has been borrowed from More, Morris has certainly rejected some central ideas, ensuring that Nowhere is quite distinct from *Utopia*.[30]

We have seen how Morris drew upon Ruskin for much of his philosophical inspiration in *News from Nowhere*, whilst it was the ideology of Marx which influenced his political agenda. The architecture within the society which Morris proposed had therefore two legitimizing meta-narratives: 'Nature' and 'historical continuity' or 'Tradition'. In so far as the proposals represented a criticism of industrialized nineteenth century society and an advocacy of the craft techniques of the Middle Ages, this corresponded with that which former societies perceived as 'naturalness' and with their reliance upon 'tradition'. By espousing similar principles Morris believed that the production of architecture might serve to re-engage the population with the land and avoid the division of labour which Ruskin so despised.

The argument for an architecture based upon craft production is therefore still valid today, only if it is legitimized not by some Ruskinian valorization of nature, but by a realization that the scaling down of production methods will allow for a more responsive (and therefore less wasteful) constructional language to develop. Whilst our built environment continues to be developed in order to generate profit, there can be no hope of replacing the industrialized techniques which offer financial economies to the developers but no social or environmental gains to the nation. That we might contemplate an architecture which begins with the need to establish a place for dwelling upon this earth, beneath these skies—a meaningful response to topography, ecology and climate—seems so simple yet so remote an idea in the context of our current consumer culture. However, this would seem to be an important and lasting possiblity which Morris has emphasized in his references to architecture in *News from Nowhere*.

ঌ 8 ঙ

A Market by the Way:
The Economics of Nowhere

ADAM BUICK

WILLIAM MORRIS DESCRIBED HIMSELF as a communist and declared his objective to be the establishment of a communist society. In calling himself a communist Morris was consciously identifying himself with a tradition which, in its written form, may be traced in modern times from Thomas More's *Utopia*[1] to the manifesto drawn up by Marx and Engels for the Communist League of Germany in 1848[2]. Morris was also aware that men and women had once lived in social conditions resembling those he wanted to see established and that vestiges of these had survived into medieval and modern times. Unfortunately, since his day the word 'communism' has become distorted to refer to the bureaucratic, class-divided societies that exist in countries such as Russia and China. This was not at all what Morris meant by communism. At most he might have regarded the period immediately following the Russian revolution as an attempt to establish the 'State Socialism' he saw as a very probable, but far from desirable, stage on the way to communism. Subsequent developments in Russia, however, would have confirmed his worst fears about the dangers of society becoming bogged down in this stage and ending up as what would now be called 'state capitalism' rather than evolving rapidly towards the 'pure Communism' described in *News from Nowhere* and which he declared to be 'the only reasonable condition of Society'.[3]

The society Morris wanted to see established was not an ideal social system which he had invented out of his own imagination. In becoming a communist Morris joined an historical tradition which already had a clear idea about the basic features of the society it advocated:

common ownership in place of private property, and, instead of buying and selling, production and distribution according to need. Morris was in fact to become one of communism's most eloquent advocates.

Morris, however, wanted to say more about communism than these bare essentials of it being a society of common ownership and distribution according to need. He wanted to bring it alive for people, as a means of getting them to want to establish it, by showing how it could function and what it could be like. His intention was not to draw up a blueprint of what communism had to be like, but merely to illustrate what it might be like. Naturally, and quite legitimately, in *News from Nowhere*, which describes a communist society that has been in existence for a number of generations, he also incorporated into this picture features which he personally wanted it to have.

Morris's personal preferences ranged from such matters as styles of dress and architecture to the non-use of machinery in agriculture and a revival of handicraft for the production of articles of everyday use. What I want to discuss in this chapter, however, is how he handled the question, which all communist writers have to face, of how the production and distribution of wealth could be organized in a society without money or coercive government.

Production for Use and the End of Buying and Selling

'The Communist', stated Morris in a lecture on Communism he delivered in 1893, 'asserts in the first place that the resources of nature, mainly the land and those other things which can only be used for the reproduction of wealth and which are the effect of social work, should not be owned in severalty, but by the whole community for the benefit of the whole. . . . The resources of nature therefore, and the wealth used for the production of further wealth, the plant and stock in short, should be communized.'[4]

Morris argued that such a community of equals, having full and free access to the means of production, would naturally use them to produce the useful things it needed to satisfy the individual and collective needs of its members. In communism, production oriented towards selling on a market with a view to profits for a privileged owning class would automatically cease, and be replaced by production directly for use. 'The whole system founded on the World Market and its supply' as he puts it in *News from Nowhere*, would disappear and be replaced by one founded instead on 'the satisfaction of the common needs of mankind and the preparation for them'.[5]

Morris saw this satisfaction of 'the common needs', or ordinary needs, of all its members, as the only rational aim of human society. He became a communist when he realized that this would only be possible on the basis of what he described as 'the workers properly organized for production' having free access to means of production as well as its fruits which they would have co-operated to make available.

The principle 'from each according to their ability, to each according to their needs' would apply: 'No other ideal on this matter of livelihood in a post-monopolist community appears to me worth considering than the satisfaction of each man's needs in return for the exercise of his faculties for the benefit of each and all: to me this seems the only rational society. And this means practical equality. For when you have satisfied the man's needs what else can you do for him?'[6]

In communism everybody would be able freely to satisfy their needs; they would not have to pay for the useful things they needed but could simply go to the stores and take them according to their own assessment of their needs. This is what happens in the communist society described in *News from Nowhere* where the Guest from the 19th century once or twice gets himself into incomprehensible situations by wanting to pay for things. Although it is not until halfway through the narrative (the end of Chapter XIV) that Morris uses the term 'communism' to describe the society existing in Nowhere, he introduces very early on (Chapter II) the fact that money is no longer used, as in the following brilliant passage. Dick Hammond has just rowed Guest across the Thames:

> He jumped out and I followed him; and of course I was not surprised to see him wait, as if for the inevitable after-piece that follows the doing of a service to a fellow-citizen. So I put my hand in my waistcoat-pocket, and said 'How much?' though still with the uncomfortable feeling that perhaps I was offering money to a gentleman. He looked puzzled, and said, 'How much? I don't

quite understand what you are asking about. Do you mean the tide? If so, it is close on the turn now.' I blushed, and said, stammering, 'Please don't take it amiss if I ask you; I mean no offence: but what ought I to pay you? You see I am a stranger, and don't know your customs—or your coins.' And therewith I took a handful of money out of my pocket, as one does in a foreign country. And by the way, I saw that the silver had oxydised, and was like a blackleaded stove in colour.

He still seemed puzzled, but not at all offended; and he looked at the coins with some curiosity. I thought, Well after all, he is a waterman, and is considering what he may venture to take. He seems such a nice fellow that I'm sure I don't grudge him a little over-payment. I wonder, by the way, whether I couldn't hire him as a guide for a day or two, since he is so intelligent. Therewith my new friend said thoughtfully: 'I think I know what you mean. You think that I have done you a service; so you feel yourself bound to give me something which I am not to give to a neighbour, unless he has done something special for me. I have heard of this kind of thing; but pardon me for saying, that it seems to us a troublesome and roundabout custom; and we don't know how to manage it. And you see this ferrying and giving people casts about the water is my business, which I would do for anybody; so to take gifts in connection with it would look very queer. Besides, if one person gave me something, then another might, and another, and so on; and I hope you won't think me rude if I say that I shouldn't know where to stow away so many mementoes of friendship.' And he laughed loud and merrily, as if the idea of being paid for his work was a very funny joke. I confess I began to be afraid that the man was mad, though he looked sane enough; and I was rather glad to think that I was a good swimmer, since we were so close to a deep swift stream. However, he went on by no means like a madman: 'As to your coins, they are curious, but not very old; they seem to be all of the reign of Victoria; you might give them to some scantily-furnished museum. Ours has enough of such coins, besides a fair number of earlier ones, many of which are beautiful, whereas these nineteenth century ones are so beastly ugly, ain't they?'[7]

Guest again gets into the same difficulty when, later on, in 'another exhibition of extinct commercial morality',[8] he asks the young girl serving in the store in Piccadilly how he will be able to pay for the tobacco pouch she offers him.

Morris had begun the chapter in which this incident occurs (Chapter VI 'A Little Shopping') as follows:

> As he spoke, we came suddenly out of the woodland into a short street of handsomely built houses, which my companion named to me at once as Piccadilly: the lower part of these I should have called shops, if it had not been that, as far as I could see, the people were ignorant of the arts of buying and selling. Wares were displayed in their finely designed fronts, as if to tempt people in, and people stood and looked at them, or went in and came out with parcels under their arms, just like the real thing.[9]

It is through these literary devices that Morris brings out the idea that communism would be a society without buying and selling and without money, in which people would have free access to goods and services according to their own self-defined needs.

Common Ownership Not Government Ownership

Within the framework of the common ownership and distribution according to needs, which have to be the basic features of any communist society, a great many decision-making arrangements are conceivable and were in fact conceived by different writers in the communist tradition. Thomas More's communism had many hierarchical features, while Etienne Cabet, in his *Voyage to Icaria*,[10] describes a communist society in which all production and distribution is controlled by a single democratically-controlled centre. Others retained the idea of control by a single centre but dropped the idea of democratic control, envisaging decisions being made by some group of experts. Edward Bellamy, whose *Looking Backward*[11] provoked Morris into writing *News from Nowhere*, had such central control being exercised by the General Council of the 'industrial army' into which he saw the workforce being organized in order to carry out production. Morris placed himself at the other end of this spectrum.

While not denying the need for a certain degree of central co-ordination, he outlined the case for a communist society of equals in which decision-making power would flow from bottom upwards rather than from the top down.

Morris was well aware that the 'equality of condition' which would exist in communism made the whole concept of property redundant. In his lecture 'How We Live and How We Might Live' he speaks of 'the people—that is, all society—duly organized, having in its own hands the means of production, to be owned by no individual, but used by all as occasion called for its use.'[12] To say that someone 'owns' something is to say that they control access to it to the exclusion of everyone else. But if everybody, either as an individual or as a member of a 'duly organized' group, has free access to the means of production, then no one is excluded; every member of society stands in the same position with regard to using the means of production. Thus it is just as accurate to say that communism is based on the non-ownership as on the common ownership of the means of production. In communism the means of production belong to no one, to no individual nor to any group or institution within society; they are simply there to be used. The concept of property is replaced by that of use; property rights in the means of production give way to commonly agreed social arrangements for allowing the members of society free access to means of production to use as and when needed.

Although Morris envisaged what he called 'state socialism' (but which Kropotkin more accurately called 'state capitalism') as a likely transitional stage on the way to communism, he was adamant that communism itself could not be based on state or government ownership. This was because he saw the state as essentially an instrument of coercion, a means of governing people, of ruling over them, which could not exist in the classless society of equals he envisaged communism as necessarily being. For him the State was the machinery of coercion (government, courts, armed forces, police, prisons) needed to enforce the monopoly exercised by the owning class over access to the means of production. It followed that the abolition of this monopoly would mean the end also of the machinery needed to enforce it and hence the disappearance of government and the State. This is very well brought out by Morris in Chapter XI of *News from*

Nowhere, 'Concerning Government', where Old Hammond explains to Guest that 'we have no longer anything which you . . . would call a government'.[13] Coercive government is replaced in communism by non-coercive 'arrangements' for settling social affairs.

In short, for Morris, communism could not be based on government ownership because there would be no government in communism. For him communism did not mean that the means of production are to be owned by an institution apart from the members of society, but rather that these means are freely available when people need to use them. In contrast to government ownership, common ownership is not a form of property, but the arrangements made to allow people full and free access to the means of production.

Morris held that in communism the coercive functions of a central government would simply disappear, while most of its purely administrative activities would be devolved to local communities and groups of producers. Morris wrote with Bax in *Socialism Its Growth and Outcome* (also originally published as a series of articles in *The Commonweal*) that after the revolution there 'should take place a gradual and increasing delegation of the present powers of central government to municipal and local bodies, until the political nation should be sapped, and give place to a federation of local and industrial organisations' which would eventually develop into 'a complete automatic system'.[14]

In his lecture 'How Shall We Live Then?'[15] Morris suggested, 'in order to give all men a share in the responsibility of the administration of things which I hope will take the place of the government of persons', that the basic 'unit of management' in communism should be the local community—'a commune, or a ward, or a parish', as he put it in *News from Nowhere*.[16] Such a relatively small unit was desirable, he argued, 'so that the greatest possible number of persons might be interested in public affairs'.[17] As Old Hammond explains in Chapter XIV of *News from Nowhere* ('How Matters Are Managed'), the decision-making body in these communities would be the general meeting ('mote') of all the members of the community; normally decisions would be taken by consensus and only as a last resort by majority vote and then only provided that all those taking part in the vote agreed to accept its result.

As no such local community could be, or would need or want to be, entirely self-sufficient, it would have to have links with others for certain purposes. Morris suggested that this be done on a federal basis, so that centralized States would come to be replaced, on a world as well as a national level, by a 'Federation of Independent Communities', 'a system of free communities living in harmonious federation with each other, managing their own affairs by the free consent of their members'.[18] As he and Bax wrote: 'The highest unit would be the great council of the socialized world, and between these would be federations of localities arranged for convenience of administration. The great federal organizing power, whatever form it took, would have the function of the administration of production in its wider sense. It would have to see to, for instance, the collection and distribution of all information as to the wants of populations and the possibilities of supplying them, leaving all details to the subordinate bodies, local and industrial'.[19]

The federal bodies would be composed of delegates from local communities and, once again, having no coercive power to impose their decisions, would normally have to reach decisions by consensus. The role of the centre would essentially be statistical, gathering information about what goods were needed and then passing this on to the appropriate bodies for them to arrange for this to be produced.

Morris and Bax went on to suggest that, just as the basic unit of administration would be the local community, so the basic industrial unit would be a local 'guild': 'Topographically, we conceive of the township as the lowest unit, industrially, of the trade or occupation organized somewhat on the lines of a craft-guild. In many instances the local branch of the guild would be within the limits of the township.'[20] So, those working in the same trade or industry would organize themselves into a body to control production in that particular branch. These industrial bodies too would federate on a national and a world basis. In one of his early lectures, 'Justice and Socialism' (1885), Morris envisaged a sort of industrial parliament to discuss and arrange such matters:

> As to what goods are required by the community that the community will settle for itself by means of any set of rational representatives whom it may select for this purpose. Nothing can possibly

be easier with any decent organization than to find out for instance whether more boots and shoes are wanted than are being made and to act accordingly. It is not moreover difficult to imagine a system by which representatives of all the trades should meet together to settle questions of trade. It must be recollected of course that there being no classes, such representatives are really so being simple members of the body they represent, and very unlike our 'members of parliament'.[21]

So Morris was suggesting, as a way of organizing decision-making and wealth production in a communist world, an administrative and industrial structure based, on the one hand, on local communities federated into regions which would send delegates to a World Council and, on the other, on the organization of productive units into local, regional and no doubt world delegate bodies according to the nature of the product concerned.

Recurring Alternative to the Capitalist World-Market

This is a radical alternative to what existed in Morris's day, and which still exists in an even more developed form in our day, and which Morris, speaking through Old Hammond described as follows:

It is clear from all that we hear and read, that in the last age of civilization men got into a vicious circle in the matter of production of wares. They had reached a wonderful facility of production, and in order to make the most of that facility they had gradually created (or allowed to grow, rather) a most elaborate system of buying and selling, which has been called the World-Market; and that World-Market, once set a-going, forced them to go on making more and more of these wares, whether they needed them or not. So that while (of course) they could not free themselves from the toil of making real necessaries, they created in a never-ending series sham or artificial necessaries, which became, under the iron rule of the aforesaid World-Market, of equal importance to them with the real necessaries which supported life. By all this they burdened themselves with a prodigious mass of work merely for the sake of keeping their wretched system going. . . . Since they had forced themselves to stagger along under this horrible burden of unnecessary production, it became impossible for them to look upon labour and its results from any other point of view than one—to wit, the ceaseless endeavour to expend the least possible amount of labour on any article made, and yet at the same time to make as many articles as possible. To this 'cheapening of production', as it was called, everything was sacrificed: the happiness of the workman at his work, nay, his most elementary comfort and bare health, his food, his clothes, his dwelling, his leisure, his amusement, his education—his life, in short—did not weigh a grain of sand in the balance against this dire necessity of 'cheap production' of things, a great part of which were not worth producing at all. . . . The whole community, in fact, was cast into the jaws of this ravening monster, 'the cheap production' forced upon it by the World-Market.[22]

Communism would end this tyranny of the world market and allow humans to escape from the vicious circle it engendered and to re-orientate production towards the satisfaction of their ordinary needs:

The wares which we make are made because they are needed: men make for their neighbours' use as if they were making for themselves, not for a vague market of which they know nothing, and over which they have no control: as there is no buying and selling, it would be mere insanity to make goods on the chance of their being wanted; for there is no longer any one who can be compelled to buy them. So that whatever is made is good, and thoroughly fit for its purpose. Nothing can be made except for genuine use; therefore no inferior goods are made. Moreover, as aforesaid, we have now found out what we want, so we make no more than we want; and as we are not driven to make a vast quantity of useless things, we have time and resources enough to consider our pleasure in making them.[23]

As Morris felt that most of these common, or ordinary needs of people—for food, clothes, housing and household goods—could and should be met locally, what he was proposing was the replacement of the world market and centralized States by an interlocking network of human-scale communities that would be largely self-reliant as far as the provision of their members' more basic needs was concerned. In other words, in Morris's vision of world communism, there would be production for local use, supplemented as necessary by transfers of essential materials and products not available everywhere between regions arranged by co-ordinating centres at regional and world levels.

Such a world society was a serious proposition even in Morris's day. His contemporary, Peter Kropotkin, argued the case for it in scientific rather than literary terms in a series of articles that appeared in *The Nineteenth Century* in 1888-90 and later published as a book under the title *Fields, Factories and Workshops*.[24] It had also been proposed previously by others in the communist tradition such as Gerrard Winstanley in the middle of the 17th century and Robert Owen earlier on in the 19th. A similar case has been made in our days by Murray Bookchin with his suggestion that humans should organize themselves for producing and living into 'eco-regions' whose size would be determined by the ecology of the area they inhabit.[25]

The structure proposed by Morris was not just a personal whim but a proposal that has come up time and again as an alternative to the capitalist world-market system. As such it is a proposal that deserves serious consideration as to whether it could work from an economic point of view: could the production and distribution of wealth be organized to satisfy human needs in a world without money and without centralized, coercive states? Before doing this, however, there is one misunderstanding concerning Morris that has to be cleared up and that concerns his attitude towards modern technology.

Because Morris himself had a personal dislike of steam-driven machinery, and makes it disappear in his vision of communism, he has been accused of advocating a return to a 'pastoral simplicity' quite inapplicable 'to the economic complexities of a modern industrial economy'.[26] This is to miss the point completely since Morris was concerned not so much with the technology of production in communism as with its purpose, but even on the level of technology critics like Thompson are wrong. Morris lived in an age whose technology was based on coal and iron. The electrical motor and the internal combustion engine had only just been invented and had not yet been applied to production; transport was by steam locomotive or horse-drawn carriage; houses and streets were lit by gas; many—in fact, most—workers still worked in small workshops rather than large factories. Morris did have a personal dislike of steam-powered machinery and naturally, in his personal account of what he would like to see develop in a communist society that had been in existence for a few generations, has it disappear. This means that there are no railways in Nowhere so that water again has become a major means of long-distance transport. But to have abolished the steam engine in 1890 would not have been to take technology back to Ancient times (to 'Arcadia') nor to Medieval times, but merely back a hundred years, to the technology existing in the middle of the 18th century— the same technology on which Adam Smith, the mentor of Thompson and other critics of communism, based his theory of the need for a profit-driven market economy.

Morris did not write so much of abolishing steam engines as of their becoming largely unnecessary (some coal is still mined in Nowhere), partly because people would prefer to make things of everyday use by hand but also partly because he foresaw that there would be a 'great change in the use of mechanical force'.[27] He did not go into much detail here, but it is clear a couple of references—to people being able to have power 'at the places where they live, or hard by'[28] and to the mysteriously-powered 'force barges'[29]—that he had in mind some form of electrical power, which is hardly a source of energy that would exist in a 'pastoral' or 'Arcadian' society.

Morris could not have foreseen—but then he was not writing a science fiction book, nor did he want to imitate the technological speculations of a Bellamy—that the application of electricity to industry under capitalism would give the coal-burning steam engine another application in that electricity came to be generated by steam-driven turbines. Nor could he have foreseen that even today no efficient system of electrical storage, such as would permit the general use of force-barges and electric cars or power at home without pylons and cables, has been invented. However, as it happens, electricity can be generated by means such as wind and water power and solar

heaters and batteries which would have been compatible with the
sort of decentralized society Morris had in mind and in fact provide
a modern technological basis for it.

Is Communism Economically Feasible?

'It's a nice idea, but it wouldn't work' is the popular objection to
pure communism and is a thought that will have occurred to many
a reader of *News from Nowhere*. A whole branch of conventional
economics exists to provide a theoretical justification for this popular
view. The basic objection is that it is impossible to organize the production and distribution of wealth, at least not without enormous
waste and inefficiency, without having recourse to money and monetary calculation. Since money, as a medium of exchange, implies the
existence of exchange and since exchange implies the existence of
products belonging to separate owners (exchange is not a physical
transfer of products but a change of ownership rights over them), to
say that you cannot abolish money is to say that you cannot abolish
private ownership and so can never establish communism.

One economist in this field, Alec Nove, has argued that the abolition of pricing, buying and selling, and monetary calculation, would
only be possible given two conditions—'absolute abundance and a
species of static equilibrium'—both of which he regards as being
unrealistic, indeed unrealizable. Given these assumptions, he writes:

> All inputs are then as abundantly and as freely available as water
> is in Scotland. Requirements, needs, inputs, techniques, are all
> known and hardly ever change. Just as the citizen will go to the
> store to collect whatever goods he or she wants, so the manage-
> ment would fetch the required steel sheet, lathes, sulphuric acid,
> cloth, pork, cabbages; that would dispose of the problem of the
> planning of inputs. The workers will then produce the output
> which 'society' or its customers require. No money would pass,
> there would be no exchange, no purchase-and-sale. So—no
> commodity production. Also no complex bureaucratic central
> planning mechanism. *Et voilà!* [30]

Actually, despite its ironic tone, this provides a clue as to how a communist society could organize the production and distribution of wealth without either the market mechanism or bureaucratic central planning: on the basis of the productive units having free access to the resources they require to produce the goods and services to meet people's needs. Communist society would have to set up an integrated structure of circuits of production and distribution at local, regional and world levels which would allow the flow of wealth to the final consumer to take place on this basis of each unit in the structure having free access to what it needed to fulfil its role. Once this had been established the system would be more or less self-regulating in the way that the market economy is supposed to be, only with productive units responding not to monetary demand but to real demand as indicated by what people actually took from the stores under conditions of free access. The role of the centre would be, as envisaged by Morris and Bax, essentially statistical. Indeed, Nove denies that this would be planning as 'the centre has no function'.[31]

Morris envisaged what people indicated they needed being recorded and acted upon by people he refers to as 'housekeepers'. As Hammond explains to Guest at the end of Chapter XII 'Concerning the Arrangement of Life':

> Although there are so many, indeed by far the greater number amongst us, who would be unhappy if they were not engaged in actually making things, and things which turn out beautiful under their hands,—there are many, like the housekeepers I was speaking of, whose delight is in administration and organization, to use long-tailed words; I mean people who like keeping things together, avoiding waste, seeing that nothing sticks fast uselessly. Such people are thoroughly happy in their business, all the more as they are dealing with actual facts, and not merely passing counters round to see what share they shall have in the privileged taxation of useful people, which was the business of the commercial folk in past days.[32]

As this passage makes clear, for Morris calculations in communist society would be done directly in physical quantities, so that not only would money not function as a means of exchange but it would not function as a unit of account either. Calculation in kind would replace monetary calculation just as free access according to need would replace buying and selling. 'Housekeeper', a translation into words of Anglo-Saxon origin of the Greek-derived word 'economist', was probably deliberately chosen by Morris (in accordance with the structure of the English language where words of Anglo-Saxon origin tend to refer to the concrete while those of Latin and Greek origin tend to refer to the abstract) to bring out the fact that such people would be concerned with concrete physical quantities rather than abstract monetary calculations. They would be stock controllers, not accountants.

Is abundance an unrealistic assumption, as Nove claims? That depends on how you define the word. The easiest definition of abundance is to say that it is the opposite of scarcity. Scarcity, however, is a relative concept in that something can only be said to be scarce in relation to the need for it. Conventional economics, which defines itself as the study of the best way to allocate scarce resources, has invented a fictional type of human being, *Homo economicus*, whose wants are limitless: an individual who always wants more and more of everything and so someone whose needs could only be satisfied if resources too were limitless. It is in relation to the needs of such fictional individuals that conventional economics defines both scarcity and abundance. Abundance, for it, is a situation where the resources for producing goods and services are available in limitless supply. Since this condition of what Nove calls 'absolute' abundance (other economists refer to it as being 'total' or 'sheer' abundance) clearly does not exist, and could only exist in some Garden of Eden where resources literally grew on trees for taking when needed, conventional economists like Nove are teaching that humanity is lumbered with scarcity as an eternal fact of economic life, indeed of the human condition, requiring recourse to pricing, buying and selling, and monetary calculation—and therefore private ownership—which too become eternal and inevitable features of economic life.

Such a definition of abundance bears no relation to the real world of real men and women engaged in transforming nature to satisfy their various socially-determined needs. For needs do not exist as the wants of some abstract individual outside society, but are always the needs of concrete individuals in a concrete social context. Quite simply, needs are not, and never have been, infinite; they are in fact relatively modest: healthy food, comfortable clothes, decent housing and all the other requirements to lead a life free from material insecurity (together with non-material needs such as being part of a genuine community and getting enjoyment from working, which a commercial society like capitalism cannnot even understand, let alone take account of).

The fact that human needs are not infinite undermines the whole theoretical basis on which conventional economics is constructed. For if needs have a limit, then the Garden of Eden definition of abundance falls and the question that has to be asked is whether or not resources are sufficient to meet, not the needs of fictional *Homo economicus*, but what Morris called 'the common needs of mankind'. Are there, or are there not, sufficient resources in the world, either actually or potentially, to satisfy the needs of every man, women and child on the planet Earth? This is not the place to set out the detailed scientific research and factual surveys which show the answer to be yes. Suffice it to say that abundance in the sense of being able to produce more than enough to satisfy Morris's common needs could exist. So Morris's assumption of there being enough resources available in a communist society for people to be able to take according to their needs is not at all unrealistic.

Because this abundance would not be 'absolute', choices, including mutually exclusive ones, would still have to be made. This would be on the basis of a direct comparison of the real concrete advantages and disadvantages of the competing projects. Thus, at Wallingford, among other things, Henry Morsom shows Guest, Ellen, Dick and Clara

> an account of a certain village council who were working hard at all this business; and the record of their intense earnestness in getting to the bottom of some matter which in time past would have seemed quite trivial as, for example, the due proportions of alkali and oil for soap-making for the village wash, or the exact heat of the water into which a leg of mutton should be plunged for boiling—all this joined to the utter absence of anything like

party feeling, which even in a village assembly would certainly have made its appearance in an earlier epoch, and was very amusing, and at the same time instructive.[33]

The examples are mundane but deliberately so, as Morris wanted to bring out the point that the various assemblies and councils that would exist in communist society would have to discuss everyday, practical problems concerning the organization of production for need (Morris's examples concern, in accordance with his personal preference of what should happen in communism, agricultural and artisanal production, but we can imagine the same sort of discussions concerning industrial production; it is the principle not the content that is important here). Decisions and choices concerning production in a communist society would be made on the basis of a direct comparison between known wants in relation to available physical resources and not on that of trying to reduce both to some abstract unit of economic value. Comparisons and calculation in real, physical terms would, here also, replace the monetary calculation of 'the commercial system'.

Conventional economics finds the idea of a steady-state economy[34] just as absurd as abundance, and for the same reason: it conflicts with its basic assumption of infinite wants. Obviously, if wants are infinite, then a situation where they are going to be satisfied, and where production can platform off is never going to be reached. The drive to make better and better use of 'scarce resources' by accumulating more, and ever more productive, instruments of production—economic growth—will continue indefinitely. Morris realized, and has Old Hammond clearly say so in News from Nowhere, that this drive towards 'the cheapening of production', with all its harmful effects on working and living conditions and on the environment, was the consequence not of human nature (Homo economicus is a myth) but of the productive system being oriented towards selling on the world market, and so would cease once production had come to be reoriented towards the direct satisfaction of local needs.

If needs are recognized as being finite, it is 'growth for growth's sake', and not a steady-state economy, that appears as the absurdity. A steady-state economy, in which production would be geared simply to meeting current needs and to replacing and repairing the existing stock of means of production (both raw materials and instruments of production), then emerges as a much more normal situation than an economy geared blindly to accumulating more and more means of production. After all, the only rational reason for accumulating means of production is eventually to be in a position fully to satisfy people's needs. Once the stock of means of production at the disposal of a society which had set itself this goal, as a communist society would, has been built up to this level, then accumulation, or the further expansion of the stock of means of production, can stop and production levels be stabilized.

It is true that today human needs are far from being met on a world scale and that a growth in the production of food, housing and other basic amenities would still be needed for some years even if production ceased to be governed by the economic laws of the capitalist world market. But since Morris is writing about a communist society that has been established for a number of generations it was again quite reasonable of him to assume that by that time production would have reached a level at which accumulation could stop and a steady-state economy come into being.

In any event, the achievement of such an economy is an ecological imperative. Humans are a part of nature, but a part that has yet to find a stable niche in the ecology of the biosphere. Such a niche has to be found as, whatever conventional economists may teach about economic growth having to continue for ever, it simply cannot. Sooner or later, humanity must establish a stable, sustainable relationship with the rest of nature, one where its needs on a world scale, and what it takes from the rest of nature to satisfy them, would be in balance with the capacity of the biosphere to renew itself after supplying them. Indeed, it is because such a balance could only be achieved within the framework of a communist society that Morris's communism remains not just a practical solution to the problem of how rationally to satisfy 'the common needs of mankind' but an urgent necessity if the human species is to survive in harmony with the rest of nature.

ಹ 9 ಲ

The Ending of the Journey:
William Morris, *News from Nowhere* and Ecology

PADDY O'SULLIVAN

THE LEGACY OF MORRIS in the fields of design, and in political theory, is well known, and acknowledged by the other authors in this book. Less often recognized is that Morris, in many of his essays and lectures, sketched out the principles of what today would be called an ecological society. In *News from Nowhere*, he described this in detail.

During the previous wave of interest in the environment, the link between Morris's ideas and environmentalism (or 'ecology') was described for example by Gould[1], but these articles failed to remove him from the artistic ghetto to which society at large has confined him since his death. In fact Morris's potential contribution to 'green' ideas and thought goes far beyond a mere aesthetic reaction to ecological disruption, and in *News from Nowhere* extends to a detailed description of the social organization, economics, and government of a small-scale, decentralized society, as well as the likely appearance of its landscape. Morris achieved this by giving consideration to the changes which his political ideas, if put into practice, would bring about, first of all in human society, but also, and no less important, in the surrounding nature (or, in modern jargon, in 'adjacent ecological systems').

Interest in such ideas, as in politics, was slow to germinate in Morris's mind. Indeed, the two themes, quite logically, go hand in hand, for in 1877, about the same time as he was busy with the Eastern Question,[2] the Society for the Preservation of Ancient Buildings (SPAB), or as Morris called it, the 'Anti-Scrape', was formed, with Morris, as ever, as Hon. Treasurer, and a membership including Burne-Jones, Carlyle, Faulkner, Holman Hunt and Webb.

Morris, however, was no mere conservationist, and had much more in store than that. As a result of his Anti-Scrape work, he began to write and deliver a series of lectures on the relationship between art and society, and it was from this, as with his eventual political stance, that his 'ecological' ideas sprang. For example, in *The Lesser Arts* (1877) he wrote

I have a sort of faith, though, that this clearing away of all art will not happen, that men will get wiser, as well as more learned; that many of the intricacies of life, on which we pride ouselves more than enough, partly because they are new, partly because they have come with the gain of better things, will be cast aside as having played their part, and being useful no longer. I hope that we shall have leisure from war—war commercial as well as war of the bullet and the bayonet; leisure from the knowledge that darkens counsel; leisure above all from the greed of money, and the craving for that overwhelming distinction that money now brings; I believe that as we have even now partly achieved LIBERTY, so we shall one day achieve EQUALITY, which, and which only, means FRATERNITY, and so leisure from poverty and all its griping, sordid cares.

Then having leisure from all these things, amidst renewed simplicity of life we shall have leisure to think about our work, that faithful daily companion, which no man any longer will venture to call the Curse of labour: for surely then we shall be happy in it, each in his place, no man grudging at another; no one bidden to be any man's *servant*, everyone scorning to be any man's *master*: men will then assuredly be happy in their work, and that happiness will assuredly bring forth decorative, noble, *popular* art.

That art will make our streets as beautiful as the woods, as elevating as the mountain-sides: it will be a pleasure and a rest, and not a weight upon the spirits to come from the open country into a town; every man's house will be fair and decent, soothing to his mind and helpful to his work: all the works of man that we live among and handle will be in harmony with nature, will be reasonable and beautiful: yet all will be simple and inspiriting, not childish and enervating; for as nothing of beauty and splendour that man's mind and hand may compass shall be wanting from our public buildings, so in no private dwelling will there be any signs of waste, pomp, or insolence, and every man will have his share of the best.[3]

One could be forgiven for interpreting this as stating only an aesthetic position, in that Morris refers constantly to art, and to beauty. However, even at this relatively early stage of the development of his political ideas, there are other themes, including simplicity of lifestyle, harmony with nature, the inherent wastefulness of the Market, and most important of all, the nature of Work. Furthermore, what Morris meant by art, was not just what would be defined by a narrow use of the word, but all of human enterprise, the production of human *artefacts*.

Morris therefore adopted an holistic view of what some environmental economists call the 'resource process'—everything that happens to a commodity from the time that it is extracted from nature to the time it is 'thrown away'. He also had a role for scientists, thus:

And Science—we have loved her well, and followed her diligently, what will she do? I fear she is so much in the pay of the counting-house, the counting-house and the drill-sergeant, that she is too busy, and for the present will do nothing. Yet there are matters which I should have thought easy for her; say for example teaching Manchester how to consume its own smoke, or Leeds how to get rid of its superfluous black dye without turning it into the river, which would be as much worth her attention as the production of the heaviest of black silks, or the biggest of useless guns. Anyhow, however it be done, unless people care about carrying on their business without making the world hideous, how can they care about Art? I know it will cost much both of time and money to better these things even a little; but I do not see how these can be better spent than in making life cheerful and honourable for others and for ourselves; and the gain of good life to the country at large that would result from men seriously setting about the bettering of decency of our big towns would be priceless, even if nothing specially good befell the arts in consequence: I do not know that it would; but I should begin to think matters hopeful if men turned their attention to such things, and I repeat that, unless they do so, we can scarcely even begin with any hope our endeavours for the bettering of the arts.[4]

So Morris, by 1877, had not only recognized pollution as the inevitable consequence of the uncaring use of nature (and not just some kind of 'accident' or 'by-product'), but had also defined a role for science in the 'care and maintenance of a small planet' that has been only generally accepted some hundred years later. The costs of the clean-up phase would be high, but how could people profess to care about Art (here used in the narrow sense), if they did not care about pollution? And as Morris defined art (in the wide sense) as all of human enterprise and human expression, then for him a society which did not care about the despoliation of nature, did not care for itself.

The most important of the above ideas, however, is the one about the nature of Work. As Morris knew, and spent most of the last third of his life explaining, the contrast between the concept of Work in a capitalist society, and in an 'ecological' society, subsumes all the other differences between them. As James Robertson[5] explains, it is a 'shift in the work paradigm' that underlies the change from the present to the Post-Industrial society.

Morris explores this theme further in *Useful Work versus Useless Toil* (1885). In this essay, he states his belief that work needs to offer the labourer three 'hopes'—hope of rest, hope of product, and hope of pleasure.

> All other work than this is worthless—it is slaves' work!—mere toiling that we may live in toil![6]

By hope of rest, Morris meant the opportunity to recover from labour, not only physically but mentally. In Victorian times this clearly referred to the long hours worked both by manual and by clerical workers. Yet nowadays, when some have too much work, and others have none, it also rings true.

Hope of product meant that work should involve the production of an article of both use and value.

> Have nothing in your houses which you do not know to be useful, or believe to be beautiful.[7]

The labour process should offer both mental and physical pleasure, and creative skill. By this Morris meant the final hope—hope of pleasure.

According to Morris, under the profit system, hope of product is squeezed, in the interests of competition. Goods may or may not be of what is understood as high quality, but always they will never be of the highest quality possible, so long as profit has to be made, and competition is the basis of the economy. Consequently, much work is devoted to unproductive tasks, so that a great deal of surplus wealth has to be produced. This, says Morris, is waste, and prevents production of goods of real value.

The way to change this is to abolish unproductive work, which would immediately confer upon most people two of the three hopes—those of rest, in the form of increased leisure, and of product, in that efforts would be concentrated upon producing only goods of value. Morris goes further, however, and states that he demands also the third hope—that of pleasure. For if getting rid of unproductive work gave rise to a surplus of labour, not only could working hours become shorter, but labour inputs to production could be increased. Work could also become more diverse—indoors and outdoors, in the workshop and in the fields. Increased leisure time would therefore lead, paradoxically, not to unemployment, but to an *increase* in the amount of work done, as Popular, or People's Art, killed as it had been by commercialism, was revived.[8]

Workplaces would also be more pleasant, as more people began to work nearer home (or as the distinction between the home and the workplace became more blurred[9]). Small workshops would replace factories. Tasks, which would become less-specialized, could therefore be rotated. Machinery would be truly labour-saving, releasing labourers from boring or arduous work, whereas at present all that 'labour-saving' devices (such as the word processor on which this is being written) achieve, is the creation of the possibility of *more* work.

In the present money economy, such measures would make goods more expensive, but their quality would be much greater, and they would have to be better produced. However, their 'price' would still not even begin to approach their true, 'ecological cost', in terms of the damage inflicted on Nature during their production, for this cannot be measured by the Market. With this point, however, Morris is not concerned, for Nowhere is a moneyless economy, and production is for need rather than demand. Instead, what he is preoccupied with is the quality of those goods produced, and the human pleasure which is derived from their production. Most salient also, in the light of recent experience with the human food chain, both in Britain and abroad, is his insistence that with the abolition of surplus value, food would become more abundant, and be of a higher quality.

Adulteration laws are only necessary in a society of thieves[10]

The similarity between these ideas and those of another great thinker and writer of the nineteenth century, Peter Kropotkin (1842-1921) is very striking. In *Fields, Factories, Workshops*,[11] Kropotkin also set out his ideas of how a free society could be organized on a rational, non-competitive basis. He described how he thought work would become less-specialized, and how settlement patterns would be changed in favour of autonomous, self-reliant industrial villages, in which manufacturing would be carried out in small workshops, and in which food would be grown in the surrounding fields, cultivated intensively using recycled urban wastes. The advantages of this type of society, thought Kropotkin, would be the integration of manual and mental labour, leading to greater work-satisfaction and self-expression; flexibility, individuality and quality of product; diversity of income and of task; greater and non-specialized skill; better living conditions; and the breakdown of divisions of class, town and country, and science and art.

Morris's ideas here also prefigure, by about a century, changes which writers such as Hazel Henderson,[12] James Robertson[13] and Walter and Dorothy Schwarz[14] believe to be happening today all over the Western world, and which are said to be heralding the arrival of the Post-Industrial Society. In particular, Morris's belief in the necessity for goods to be of the highest possible quality, so that they will last for as long as possible, (which also minimises the ecological damage involved in their production) and be beautiful and satisfying to make (so as to allow for individual human expression), is a mainstream 'green' idea. That Morris arrived at this position from an independent understanding of what he later found had been called by Marx the 'Theory of Surplus Value', is documented by Thompson.[15]

The advantages of such a society, says Morris, would be good health (freedom from the diseases both of poverty and of surfeit); good, liberal education in both practical and mental skills, and not just for a specialized role (advocates of the idea that education should serve only the needs of industry, please note!); real leisure (i.e. the freedom to express oneself, whether in 'work' or some other activity); freedom to travel (but, like the travelling craft workers of the Middle Ages, to real communities, not just to resorts), and last, but not least, a healthy, unpolluted and pleasant environment of small communities, pleasant workshops, clean air and water, decent housing, gardens, fields and woods. Underlying all would be a sense of *community*.

It is in *News from Nowhere* that the above ideas are most fully worked out. In the new society, goods are made only for use, and work has become a pleasure. There has been a great revival of craft skills, and the decorative arts. As old Hammond tells Guest,[16] it was the ending of the distinction between work and leisure which made all the other changes possible. The 'incentive' to work in order to survive has therefore been replaced by the ability of work to provide pleasurable labour. There are, of course, some unpleasant jobs for which volunteers are needed, but as this kind of work is getting scarce, there is no shortage of such people. Most manufacturing is performed in small workshops, where goods are made mainly by hand. Machines are still used (it just isn't true that Morris was 'against' machines), but only where there is *more* pleasure to be had in using them than in performing tasks by hand, or where the labour involved would otherwise be too great.

Where factories are necessary, in that some article has to be made on a larger scale, or where large amounts of energy can be conserved by collective enterprise, then such factories (or 'banded workshops') are built. Here people, both men and women, collect to work together, to produce for example metal (which needs smelting), and pottery and glass (which need large kilns). In such collective enterprises there is sometimes competition—to see how much work the group can perform in a given time!

Minerals are brought to the surface with as little pollution as possible,[17] and Morris hints at, but does not explicitly describe, the widespread use both of wind and water power, and of electricity, the latter presumably mainly generated by the former. Quite what method of propulsion the barges moving silently upstream on the Thames[18] employ, is not stated, however, so that whilst *News from Nowhere* does contain examples of true Alternative Technology (that technology which liberates individuals from control over their lives by others or by the state), its precise nature in some respects remains a mystery.

In the matter of the distribution of goods, there is what anthropologists would call 'free, unstratified, redistributive exchange'.[19] In other words produce is brought to market, and each person selects their requirements on the basis of need. No one is prevented from taking less than they desire, but there is no point in taking more than is needed, for there will be more tomorrow.[20] Hence, in *News from Nowhere*, Morris describes how production for needs rather than wants would satisfy the requirements of a semi-urban society, whilst also eliminating surplus value. And it is the removal of surplus production which enables the society of Nowhere to lighten the pressure it exerts upon the rest of nature. Hence Morris identifies the issue of 'needs v. wants' which underlies much of the debate not only about competitive versus collective models of society, but also the possibility of realizing a truly ecological society without resorting to extreme authoritarian rules and customs[21] (which would, of course, have been anathema to Morris).

For some environmentalists,[22] perhaps the most immediate appeal of *News from Nowhere* is that it describes in some detail, the landscape of England under a different kind of society. Much of London has changed beyond all recognition. The Essex marshes have returned to their medieval grass, and almost everywhere to the east of Aldgate—the old East End—has been demolished. Hammersmith has become an area of meadows and intensive garden agriculture (*à la* Kropotkin), and Kensington, Notting Hill and Primrose Hill a wood reaching as far as Paddington. Piccadilly still has shops, and has become a market where fine goods may be had (free!). 'Rough goods' are stored in the large buildings about the city, so that

'Westminster Market' turns out to be the old Houses of Parliament, which are now used as a manure store.[23]

Other parts of London have become orchards. The big buildings of the old central business district (the City) have been turned into commune houses. Outside London, the large industrial towns have gone, but the smaller towns have mostly remained, especially the old medieval ones which Morris clearly considered more 'organic'. Soon after the revolution, townspeople flocked to the country, and after many 'false starts', learned how to live there. In one of the most (justifiably) famous passages from the book, the landscape of the new England is described thus:

> This is how we stand. England was once a country of clearings amongst the woods and wastes, with a few towns interspersed, which were fortresses for the feudal army, markets for the folk, gathering places for the craftsmen. It then became a country of huge and foul workshops and fouler gambling-dens, surrounded by an ill-kept, poverty-stricken farm, pillaged by the masters of the workshops. It is now a garden, where nothing is wasted, and nothing is spoilt, with the necessary dwellings, sheds, and work-shops scattered up and down the country, all trim and neat and pretty. For indeed, we should be too much ashamed of ourselves if we allowed the making of goods, even on a large scale, to carry with it the appearance, even, of desolation and misery. Why, my friend, those housewives we were talking of just now would teach us better than that.
>
> Our villages are something like the best of places, with the church or mote-house of the neighbours for their chief building. Only note that there are no tokens of poverty about them: no tumbledown picturesque: which, to tell you the truth, the artist usually availed himself of to veil his incapacity for drawing architecture. Such things do not please us, even when they indi-cate no misery. Like the medievals, we like everything trim and clean, orderly and bright; as people always do when they have any sense or architectural power; because then they know that they can have what they want, and they won't stand any nonsense from Nature in their dealings with her.

Except in the wastes and forests and amongst the sand-hills (like Hindhead in Surrey), it is not easy to be out of sight of a house: and where the houses are thinly scattered they run large, and are more like the old colleges than ordinary houses as they used to be. That is done for the sake of society, for a good many people can dwell in such houses, as the country dwellers are not necessarily husbandmen; though they almost all help in such work at times. The life that goes on in these big dwellings in the country is very pleasant, especially as some of the most studious men of our time live in them, and altogether there is a great variety of mind and mood in them which brightens and quickens the society there.

The population is pretty much the same as it was at the end of the nineteenth century; we have spread it, that is all. Of course, also, we have helped to populate other countries—where we were wanted and were called for.

We like pieces of wild nature, and can afford them, so we have them; let alone that as to the forests, we need a great deal of timber, and suppose that our sons and sons' sons will do the like. As to the land being a garden, I have heard that they used to have shrubberies and rockeries in gardens once; and though I might not like artificial ones, I assure you that some of the natural rockeries of our garden are worth seeing. Go north this summer and look at the Cumberland and Westmorland ones—where, by the way, you will see some sheep feeding, so that they are not so wasteful as you think: not so wasteful as forcing-grounds for fruit out of season, I think. Go and have a look at the sheep-walks high up on the slopes between Ingleborough and Pen-y-gwent, and tell me if you think we *waste* the land there by not covering it with factories for making things that nobody wants, which was the chief business of the nineteenth century.[24]

The population of this landscape is about forty million, which is what the population of England was in 1890. The reason why they can live there on a nationally self-reliant basis, is because they no longer have to produce surplus goods. No resources are wasted.

Morris is well aware of the likely effects of these changes on other organisms, and on ecosystems. As well as the growing up of the woods and forests, there has been a definite improvement in the quality of the air, and the water in the rivers. To Victorians, perhaps one of the most dramatic changes described in *News from Nowhere* would have been that in Central London, where there is now a thriving salmon fishery.[25] The clarity of the water in the Thames tells us that upstream there are not only fewer polluting factories, but that also, somewhere, there are forests.

Birds of prey have become much more common, and the hay and corn fields are planted with scattered trees, usually fruit trees. Harvesting such fields would be entirely feasible, so long as large, cumbersome machinery was not employed. There is pollarding and coppicing of trees to provide vernacular wood, but on a careful rotation, so as not to disturb the habitat much. Many pieces of wild nature are preserved, so that people, especially young people, can use them as recreation areas, and experience wilderness. Waterways have once more become important as major transport routes.

It is in *News from Nowhere* that Morris produced his most powerful piece of writing, both from a political and ideological point of view, and from the standpoint of his influence upon modern environmentalism. Here, Morris showed how ideas and concepts developed in the arts and the humanities in the eighteenth and nineteenth centuries could be used to develop a coherent model of how a collectivist society might transform not only the lives of individuals, but whole landscapes as well. It is this aspect of *News from Nowhere* that modern radical environmentalists such as Henderson,[26] Pepper[27] and Robertson[28] have latched on to, and held up as an example of what a non-authoritarian ecological society would be like.

The central thesis is that by abolishing the production of surplus value, the new society was able to lessen its impact on the rest of nature, by a very considerable amount. Also, by adopting a new concept of the nature of Work, the society of Nowhere achieved many other things long advocated by environmentalists—particularly the conservation of energy and material resources—by slowing down the rate at which they are converted from the 'raw' state to waste. All this resulted in a new relationship with the rest of nature, and produced major landscape and ecological change.

The nature of modern environmentalism, as a social movement, has been comprehensively described by the geographer Timothy O'Riordan.[29] He divides environmentalists into technocentrists, who are basically professional and élitist in character, and ecocentrists, who are found at the 'grass-roots', and who mistrust technocentrism for its scientistic and managerial tendencies, which they see as centralizing and undemocratic.[30] Needless to say, it is upon ecocentrism, with its rejection of the complexity of modern life, and its advocacy of 'smallness' (in the sense used by the late Fritz Schumacher[31]), that the influence of Morris has been stronger.

Within ecocentrism, however, there are also at least two more contrasting strains, namely what O'Riordan calls *communalism*, in which the emphasis is upon participatory democracy, and on *human* liberation alongside that of Nature, and *gaianism*,[32] in which human aspirations are considered to be only of equal importance to, or sometimes secondary to, the demands, and the rights, of other species, and of wild ecosystems.[33] Morris, with his essential humanity, and his celebration of human skill, and human ingenuity, even though he recognized the importance of nature for the well-being of the human psyche,[34] belongs firmly in the communalist camp. In particular, he would have rejected vehemently the authoritarian tendencies which are creeping in to some forms of naturalistic ecocentrism.[35]

At the same time, *News from Nowhere* prefigures the use of 'alternative technology',[36] and in Nowhere such technology, besides being small in scale, is indeed *truly* alternative, in that it not only disperses production and therefore reduces pollution, but also gives back to the people what they had been deprived of under the centralized, capitalist state—control over their own lives. This is in fact the test of a true alternative technology.[37]

Similarly, the economy of Nowhere, as explained earlier by Adam Buick, is a true steady state economy.[38] Production is for needs, not wants, and the rate at which goods flow through the economy is reduced by making them long-lasting and of high quality. Moreover, Morris showed how, by the use of decentralized socialism, a steady state, or spaceship economy, could be successfully run *without* resorting to the brigand state of which Boulding has warned.[39]

What Morris did was to take Marxism, and apply it to the practical realities of everyday life. In doing so, he hoped to show how we could, if we wished, rid our lives of certain social evils. What he also achieved, by no means incidentally, is to provide radical environmentalists with a document setting out many of their basic ideas, in plain English, which then also explored in quite considerable detail how these would actually operate in a future society. In this way, Morris made an unrivalled contribution both to revolutionary thought, and to environmentalism.

ಜ NOTES ಜ.

(All page references to News from Nowhere *relate to the edition published in 1973 by Lawrence and Wishart, London, edited by A. L. Morton.)*

PREFACE

1 Oscar Wilde, *Plays, Prose Writings and Poems* (London: 1930) p. 270.
2 'Art Under Plutocracy' in *Political writings of William Morris*, ed. A.L. Morton (London: 1973) p. 85.
3 E.Belfort Bax and W.Morris, *Socialism: Its Growth and Outcome* (London: 1893) p. 321.
4 'The Society of the Future' in A.L.Morton, ed., op. cit.
5 'The Policy of Abstention' in *William Morris, Artist, Writer, Socialist*, ed. May Morris (Oxford: 1936) Vol. II, p. 451.
6 'The End and the Means' in *William Morris, Artist, Writer, Socialist*, ed. May Morris (Oxford: 1936) Vol. II, p. 420.

INTRODUCTION

1 J.Lindsay *William Morris, his life and works* (Constable, 1975).
2 Letter to Andreas Scheu, 5 September 1883, quoted in A.Briggs, ed. *William Morris, News from Nowhere, and Selected Writings and Designs* (Penguin).
3 G.B.Burne-Jones *Memorials of Edward Burne-Jones* (1904) vol 1, pp. 114-115, quoted in E.P.Thompson *William Morris: Romantic to Revolutionary* (Merlin, 1976).
4 J.Ruskin 'The Nature of Gothic' Chapter VI, Volume II of *The Stones of Venice* (London: Smith Elder, 1853).

5 E.P. Thompson ibid.
6 J. Marsh *Jane and May Morris: a biographical story 1839-1938* (London: Pandora, 1986).
7 May Morris *William Morris, Artist, Writer, Socialist* (2 vols) (New York: Russell & Russell, 1934).
8 E.P. Thompson op. cit.
9 J. Lindsay op. cit.
10 J.W. Mackail *The Life of William Morris* (2 vols) (Longman, 1899).
11 A. Vallance *William Morris : His Art, His Writings and His Politics* (London: George Bell & Sons, 1897; republished 1986, London: Studio Editions).
12 J. Marsh *Pre-Raphaelite Sisterhood* (London: Quartet, 1985).
13 E.P. Thompson op. cit.
14 P. Fitzgerald, ed. *The Novel on Blue Paper by William Morris* (London & New York: The Journeyman Press, 1982).
15 'Art and Socialism'(1884) in A.L. Morton, ed. *The Political Writings of William Morris* (London: Lawrence & Wishart, 1984).
16 'To The Working Men of England' reproduced in Appendix II to P. Henderson, ed. *The Letters of William Morris to his Family and Friends* (London: Longmans, Green & Co, 1950).
17 Quoted in A.L. Morton op. cit., Introduction, p. 23.
18 M. Morris op. cit.
19 'How I became a socialist'(1894) in A.L. Morton, op. cit.
20 'The Lesser Arts' (1877) in A.L. Morton, op.cit.
21 'The Art of the People' (1879) quoted in A.L. Morton op. cit. Introduction, p. 13.
22 W. Morris *Hopes and Fears for Art* (London: 1882).
23 'Useful Work versus Useless Toil' in A.L. Morton op. cit.
24 'The Lesser Arts' in A.L. Morton op. cit.
25 'How we live, and how we might live' in A.L. Morton op. cit.
26 J. Marsh *Jane and May Morris*, op. cit.
27 E.P. Thompson op. cit.
28 'The Message of the March Wind' from *The Pilgrims of Hope (1883-1886)* reprinted in A.L. Morton, ed. *Three Works by William Morris* (New York: International Publishers, 1968).
29 E.P. Thompson op. cit.

30 W. Morris (1886) *A Dream of John Ball* reprinted in A.L. Morton, ed. *Three Works by William Morris* (New York: International Publishers, 1968).

31 'Socialism and Anarchism' in A.L. Morton, ed. *The Political Writings of William Morris* (London: Lawrence & Wishart).

32 P. Kropotkin *Fields, Factories and Workshops: or Industry combined with Agriculture and Brain Work with Manual Work* (London: 1899).

33 G. Woodcock *Anarchism. A History of Libertarian Ideas and Movements* (Pelican, 1962, 1st edition).

34 E. Bellamy *Looking Backward* (1889), republished by Harmondsworth (1986).

35 'Looking Backward' by William Morris *(The Commonweal,* 22 June 1889.

36 S. Coleman 'The Economics of Utopia: Morris and Bellamy contrasted', *J. William Morris Soc.* VIII(2), 2-6, (1989).

37 *N.F.N.* p. 391

38 G.B. Shaw 'William Morris as I knew him' (1934) in M. Morris op. cit.

39 M. Morris op. cit.

40 G.B. Shaw ibid.

41 E.P. Thompson op. cit.

42 Ibid.

43 D. Ottewill *The Edwardian Garden* (New Haven & London: Yale University Press 1989).

44 P.E. O'Sullivan 'Environmental Science and environmental philosophy. II Environmental Science and the coming social paradigm.' *International Journal of Environmental Studies* 28, 257-267 (1987).

45 J.W. Mackail op. cit.

46 Robert Blatchford in the *Clarion,* October 1896.

47 E.P. Thompson op. cit.

1 Cited in E.P.Thompson *William Morris: Romantic to Revolutionary* (Merlin, 1977) p. 244.
2 Morris *A Dream of John Ball* (Lawrence & Wishart, 1973) p. 103.
3 A.L.Morton *The English Utopia* (Lawrence & Wishart, 1978) p. 208.
4 Ibid., p. 44.
5 Ibid., p. 12.
6 Ibid., pp. 15-45.
7 Ibid., p. 17.
8 Ibid., p. 44.
9 For sources and background to the Peasants' Revolt, see my *Radical Reader* (Penguin, 1984) pp. 49-68. John Ball, the heretic Kentish priest, was executed at St. Albans; Wat Tyler, leader of the Revolt, was killed at Smithfield. The Lollards were followers of John de Wycliffe (1328-84), who is said to have been an influence on the Revolt. Jack Cade led a rising of the poor against oppression in June-July 1450 which briefly took possession of London. He is dealt with unsympathetically by Shakespeare in Henry VI Part II. John Skelton (1460?-1529) was the major poet of early Tudor England. *Vox Populi Vox Dei* was an anonymous poem of the 1530s. The *Chronicle* of Edward Hall (1498?-1547) covers the history of England from Henry IV to Henry VIII. William Tyndale (1496?-1536), translator of the first English printed bible (two copies of which remain, the rest having been publicly burnt), was killed as a heretic. Robert Kett and his brother William were small landowners; they led the great Norfolk Revolt in 1549, the most significant rising of the people since the Peasants' Revolt, and took control of Norwich for three weeks. The Ketts were executed as traitors. The *Annales of England* by John Stow (1525?-1605), added to by E.Howe to 1631, records the 'Captain Pouch' rebellion, a major rising of the Midland poor in 1607.
10 A.L.Morton, op. cit., p. 77.
11 'The Hopes of Civilization', in A.L.Morton, ed. *Political Writings of William Morris* (Lawrence & Wishart, 1973), p. 165.

12 Milton *Paradise Lost* Book XII, 548-51.

13 Op. cit., p. 165.

14 For Gerrard Winstanley, see *The World Turned Upside Down* by Christopher Hill (Penguin, 1975), and Winstanley's *The Law of Freedom and other writings*, ed. Christopher Hill (Penguin, 1973). There are substantial extracts in my *Radical Reader* (Penguin 1984).

15 A. L. Morton, op. cit., p. 157.

16 E. P. Thompson, op. cit., pp. 10-11.

17 Ibid., p. 14.

18 Shelley: Notes to 'Queen Mab', in *Poetical Works* (Oxford, 1934).

19 Shelley: Preface to 'The Revolt of Islam', ibid., p. 33.

20 Shelley: 'Queen Mab', ibid., p. 772.

21 Shelley: 'Ode to the West Wind', ibid., p. 579.

22 William Holman Hunt, painter (1827-1910), Sir John Everett Millais, painter (1829-1896), Dante Gabriel Rossetti, poet and painter (1828-1882), Sir Edward Burne-Jones, painter (1833-1898).

23 E. P. Thompson, op. cit., pp. 55-6.

24 'Art & Socialism', in A. L. Morton, op. cit., p. 111.

25 E. P. Thompson, op. cit., p. 242.

26 E. P. Thompson, op. cit., pp. 798-9.

27 John Goode: 'William Morris and the Dream of Revolution', in *Literature and Politics in the 19th Century,* ed. John Lucas (Methuen, 1971) p. 278.

28 E. P. Thompson: op. cit., 172.

29 Philip Henderson *William Morris: his life, work and friends* (Penguin, 1967) p. 116.

30 Cited in E. P. Thompson, op. cit., p. 120.

31 E. P. Thompson, op. cit., p. 118.

32 Marx *Grundrisse* (Penguin, 1973) p. 452.

33 'How I Became a Socialist', in A. L. Morton, op. cit., pp. 244-5.

34 Ibid., p. 245.

35 'How We Live and How We Might Live', ibid., p. 158.

36 'Art Under Plutocracy', ibid., p. 80.

37 Marx op. cit., p. 162.

38 E. P. Thompson, op. cit., p. 244.
39 Morris *News from Nowhere* (Lawrence & Wishart, 1973) p. 288.
40 John Goode, op. cit., pp. 238-9.
41 *N.F.N.*, pp. 337-8.
42 'How We Live and How We Might Live', in A. L. Morton, op. cit., p. 154.
43 'Communism', ibid., p. 229.

2 · HOW THE CHANGE CAME

1 William Morris *News from Nowhere* (London: Lawrence & Wishart, 1973) p. 292.
2 Ibid., p. 290.
3 Ibid., pp. 293-4.
4 Ibid., p. 295.
5 Ibid., p. 295.
6 Ibid., p. 296.
7 Ibid., p. 296.
8 Ibid., p. 297.
9 Ibid., p. 304.
10 Ibid., p. 304.
11 Ibid., p. 305.
12 Ibid., p. 305.
13 Ibid., p. 305.
14 Ibid., p. 308.
15 Ibid., p. 312.
16 Ibid., p. 312.
17 Ibid., p. 313.
18 Ibid., p. 314.
19 Ibid., p. 288.
20 Ibid., p. 290.
21 Ibid., p. 304.
22 Karl Marx *Selected Works* (London: Lawrence & Wishart, 1947) vol. I, p. 107.

23 Morris, op. cit., p. 309.

24 Ibid., p. 309.

25 Ibid., p. 309.

26 Ibid., p. 291.

27 Ibid., p. 313.

28 Ibid., p. 304 (italics as in original).

29 Ibid., p. 268.

30 Ibid., p. 268.

31 Ibid., p. 293.

32 Ibid., p. 293.

33 Ibid., p. 294.

34 Ibid., p. 292.

35 Ibid., p. 298.

36 Ibid., p. 291.

37 Ibid., p. 307.

38 Ibid., p. 310.

3 · HOW MATTERS ARE MANAGED

1 *News from Nowhere*, p. 225.

2 Ibid., p. 197.

3 Ibid., p. 332.

4 Ibid., p. 395.

5 Ibid., p. 207.

6 Ibid., p. 203.

7 Ibid., pp. 185-6.

8 Ibid., p. 330.

9 Ibid., p. 371.

10 Ibid., p. 390.

11 Ibid., p. 318.

12 Ibid., p. 239.

13 Ibid., p. 286.

14 Ibid., p. 254.

15 There is no basic difference between the Judeo-Christian and the Islamic conception of human nature. I refer here to the

Judeo-Christian tradition because it is of most relevance to Western utopian thought.

16 St Augustine *City of God*, Book XIII, chap. 14, pp. 278-9 (ed. V.J. Bourke, New York: 1958).

17 John Calvin *Institutes of the Christian Religion*, Vol. I, p. 255 (London: 1961).

18 *The English Works of Thomas Hobbes*, Vol. VII, p. 73 (Molesworth: 1839).

19 Roger Scruton *The Meaning of Conservatism*, p. 99 (London: 1980).

20 Roald Dahl in *The Guardian*, 12 August 1989.

21 Katherine Whitehorn in *The Observer*, 10 October 1967.

22 'A Triumph of Human Nature' in *The Sunday Times*, 11 June 1989.

23 Quoted in George Boas, *Essays on Primitivism and Related Ideas in the Middle Ages*, p. 159 (New York: 1978).

24 Ibid., p. 165.

25 'How We Live And How We Might Live' in A.L. Morton, ed. *Political Writings of William Morris*, p. 136 (London: 1973).

26 Ibid., p. 143.

27 'What Socialists Want' in Eugene D. Lemire, ed. *The Unpublished Lectures of William Morris*, p. 217 (Detroit: 1969).

28 See E.P. Thompson *William Morris: Romantic to Revolutionary*, pp. 699-700 (London: 1977).

29 *N.F.N.*, p. 245.

30 Ibid., p. 247.

31 Ibid., p. 367.

32 Ibid., p. 189.

33 Ibid., p. 67.

34 Thomas More *Utopia*, pp. 123-4 (Harmondsworth: 1965).

35 E. Belfort Bax and William Morris *Socialism: Its Growth and Outcome*, p. 209 (London: 1893).

36 Robert Owen *A New View of Society and other Writings*, p. 14, ed. G.D.H. Cole (London: 1927).

37 *N.F.N.*, pp. 209-210.

38 Ibid., p. 209.

39 Ibid., p. 263.

40 Ibid., p. 263.
41 Ibid., p. 262.
42 Ibid., p. 266.
43 Ibid., p. 265.
44 A good example of this critique of psychiatry can be found in Thomas S. Szasz *Ideology and Insanity—Essays on the Psychiatric Dehumanization of Man* (London: 1973).
45 *N.F.N.*, pp. 353.
46 'The Society of the Future' in A.L. Morton, ed. *Political Writings of William Morris*, p. 192 (London: 1973).
47 *N.F.N.*, p. 240.
48 Ibid., p. 257.
49 Ibid., pp. 360-4.
50 Ibid., p. 401.

4 · THE OBSTINATE REFUSERS

1 H. Sparling *The Kelmscott Press and William Morris Master Craftsman* (London: Macmillan, 1924). Facsimile reprint (London: Dawson, 1975).
2 R. Noonan ('Robert Tressell') *The Ragged-Trousered Philanthropists*, 1st edition (London: Grant Richards, 1914). Standard edition ed. F. Ball (London: Lawrence & Wishart, 1955).
3 See current DSS regulations concerning the 'award' of supplementary benefit!
4 *N.F.N.* p. 226.
5 *N.F.N.* p. 227.
6 *N.F.N.* p. 227.
7 *N.F.N.* pp. 227-8.
8 *N.F.N.* pp. 349-50.
9 *N.F.N.* p. 385.
10 *N.F.N.* pp. 277-80.
11 *N.F.N.* p. 365.
12 *N.F.N.* pp. 107-8.
13 *N.F.N.* p. 367.

14 W. Morris *The Decorative Arts: their relation to modern life and progress* (London: Ellis & White. Not dated but January 1878.)

15 The Trades Guild of Learning was being formed in 1873, in which year Morris was approached by Frederic Every, a radical artisan unknown to him but perhaps not to George Campfield his foreman. The Guild was promoted by Professor George Warr (positivist and feminist) of the University of London. Every was also active in the EQA, and through him Morris met the working class and trade union leaders of that agitation which met at least once at Queen Square . . .

16 J. Ruskin *The Stones of Venice*, vol. II, (London: Smith Elder, 1853). 'On the Nature of Gothic' is Chapter VI, pp. 151-231 in the 1st edition, but one section was held over to Vol. III, Chapter III (see note 17).

17 Kelmscott Press reprint of 'The Nature of Gothic'. Preface dated February 1892. Printed at the Kelmscott Press, but published by Ruskin's publisher, George Allen, not by Morris.

Morris bought and read *The Stones of Venice* as it appeared, but his attention would be particularly directed to this chapter by the earlier reprint of October 1854. When the Workingmen's College was being set up in that year, F. J. Furnivall, who like Morris married a working-class woman, and who was much closer to working folk than F. D. Maurice, went to Ruskin, asking permission to reprint this chapter as a pamphlet to be put into the hand of everybody who attended the inaugural address on 30th October. Ruskin readily agreed, and also agreed to take a drawing class—not hitherto proposed. The sub-title 'and herein of the true functions of the Workman in Art' is not in Ruskin's original (though the words may be his), but was introduced by Furnivall, who also sought out, and attached to the pamphlet the significant part of Ruskin's text which had been deferred to Volume III, the sections on *Play*. Morris used neither the subtitle, nor the added text—a pity.

18 J. Ruskin *Unto This Last* (London: Smith Elder, 1862).

19 *Fraser's Magazine*, published at intervals from June 1862 to January 1863, and in volume as *Munera Pulveris*, George Allen (1872).

20 J.Ruskin *Fors Clavigera: Letters to Working Men.* Published monthly by George Allen between January 1871 and December 1877, and 1878-1884.

21 J.Ruskin *op. cit.* note 18.

22 See note 17.

23 J.Ruskin *The Stones of Venice.* Volume III, chapter III.

24 As 23.

25 'The Story of the Unknown Church' in *The Early Poems and Prose Romances of William Morris* (London: Everyman, 1907) but facsimile reprinted P. Faulkner, ed. (Dent 1973) pp. 141-149.

26 As 25, pp. 72-77.

27 J.Ruskin *Unto This Last* (see note 17) Essay 1: sections 11-17.

28 F.Booker *The Industrial Archaeology of the Tamar Valley* (Newton Abbot: David & Charles, 1969).

29 See note 5.

30 William Morris to Georgiana Burne-Jones, 1st June 1884. In P.Henderson, ed. *The Letters of William Morris to his Family and Friends* (London: Longmans, Green & Co., 1950).

5 · CONCERNING LOVE

The author of this chapter would like to thank Florence Boos, Norman Kelvin and Linda Richardson for their comments on her text, and for their own complementary studies of William Morris's works.

1 Friedrich Engels, *Der Ursprung der Familie, des Privateigenthums und des Staats* (Zurich: 1884, revised 1891). I have used the English language edition *The Origin of the Family, Private Property and the State* (London: 1940) p. 59.

Strictly speaking, Engels appropriated for Marxist purposes arguments from Lewis Morgan's *Ancient Society* (London: 1877) which forms the basis for *The Origin of the Family.* Although the latter text was not published in English until 1902, Engels's ideas were widely circulated, by Eleanor Marx among

others, within the Socialist movement in Britain during the 1890s.
There is some debate about how familiar Morris was in general
with Engels's unpublished work, to which his own frequently
seems to refer, but his two-part article on 'The Development of
Modern Society', published in *The Commonweal* in July and
August 1890, which summarized parts of Engels's argument in
The Origin of the Family, indicates a fairly close acquaintance
with the book, perhaps gained through discussion as Engels
revised the text. Possibly, however, Morris was more familiar
with Lewis's book than Engels's.

2 Ibid., pp. 78-80.

3 Ibid., pp. 81 & 89.

4 Ibid., pp. 89-90.

5 August Bebel, *Woman in the Past, Present and Future*, translated
   by H.B. Adams Walther (London: 1885) pp. 229-232.

6 Edward and Eleanor Marx Aveling *The Woman Question* (London: 1886) p. 15.

7 William Morris to G. Bernard Shaw, 18.3.1885, *The Collected
   Letters of William Morris*, edited Norman Kelvin (Princeton, 1987) vol. II, p. 404.

8 Ibid., II, p. 857.

9 William Morris to J. Bruce Glasier 24.4.1886, *Letters*, II, p. 545.

10 Ibid.

11 *N.F.N.*, p. 193.

12 Ibid., p. 198.

13 Ibid., p. 241.

14 Ibid., pp. 241-2.

15 Engels, op. cit., p. 50.

16 *N.F.N.*, p. 243

17 Ibid., pp. 236-7.

18 Ibid., p. 238.

19 William Morris to Aglaia Coronio, 25. 11. 1872. *Letters*, I, p. 173.

20 *N.F.N.*, p. 239

21 Ibid., p. 371.

22 Ibid., p. 322.

23 Ibid., p. 379.

24 Ibid., p. 377.
25 Ibid., pp. 383-4.
26 Ibid., p. 391.
27 Ibid., p. 399.
28 E.P. Thompson, *William Morris : Romantic to Revolutionary* ,
     2nd edn. (London: 1976) pp. 790-1; the essay quoted is from
     Miguel M-H. Abensour, *Utopies et dialectique du socialisme*
     (Paris: 1977).

FURTHER READING
Feminist and gender issues in relation to William Morris and *News
from Nowhere* have been explored by a number of scholars in recent
years; published work includes the following:

Norman Kelvin, 'The Erotic in *News from Nowhere* and *The Well
at the World's End*', *Studies in the Late Romances of William Morris*,
ed. Carole Silver and Joseph R. Dunlap, William Morris Society (New
York: 1976).

Florence Boos, 'An (Almost) Egalitarian Sage: William Morris's Later
Writings and the "Woman Question"', *Victorian Sages and the
Feminine: Gender, Discourse and Power*, ed. Thaïs Morgan (Rutgers
University Press, 1990).

Linda Richardson, 'Louise Michel and William Morris', *Journal of
the William Morris Society*, vol VIII, no. 2, Spring 1989. Richardson
further discussed William Morris's relations with socialist women in
her lecture 'Daintily-Fashioned Engines of War: William Morris and
Women of the Socialist Movement', William Morris Society, March
1987, and in her doctoral dissertation 'William Morris and Women:
Experience and Representation' (University of Oxford, 1989).

6 · AN OLD HOUSE AMONGST NEW FOLK

1 Conversation with Carl Feiss, Pittsburgh, 5 March 1988.

2 Raymond Unwin in *The Labour Leader* 18 January 1902, p. 21, quoted in Mark Swenarton *Artisans and Architects: The Ruskinian Tradition in Architectural Thought* (Macmillan, 1989).

3 Mark Swenarton ibid. citing 'W. R. Lethaby, An Impression and a Tribute' in *RIBA Journal*, Vol 39 No. 8, 20 February 1932, p. 304.

4 Raymond Unwin in *The Commonweal* 15 June 1889, p. 190, quoted in Mark Swenarton op. cit.

5 Ebenezer Howard 'Spiritual Influences Towards Social Progress' in *Light*, 30 April 1910, quoted in Robert Beevers *The Garden City Utopia, A Critical Biography of Ebenezer Howard* (Macmillan, 1988).

6 Marie Louise Berneri *Journey Through Utopia* (Routledge & Kegan Paul, 1950; new edition Freedom Press, 1986) p. 259.

7 *N.F.N.* pp. 390-1.

8 Michael Hughes, ed. *The Letters of Lewis Mumford and Frederic J. Osborn* (Adams and Dart, 1971) p. 143.

9 William Morris Preface to *The Nature of Gothic* in May Morris *William Morris: Artist, Writer, Socialist* (Oxford University Press, 1936) Vol I, p. 292.

10 Hermann Muthesius *Das Englische Haus* (Berlin: Ernst Wasmuth, 3 Vols 1904-1905). English translation *The English House* (1979) p. 13.

11 Mark Swenarton op. cit. p. 202.

12 William Morris *Works* Vol XVI pp. 71-72, quoted in Paul Thompson *The Work of William Morris* (2nd edition, Quartet Books, 1977) p. 278.

13 William Morris ibid. Vol. XXIII p. 22, quoted in Paul Thompson ibid. p. 73. (A 3rd edition of Thompson's book will be published by Oxford University Press in 1990).

14 David Lea 'One Earth: William Morris's Vision' in *William Morris Today* (London: Institute of Contemporary Arts, 1984) p. 57.

15 John McKean *Learning from Segal* (Basle: Birkhäuser Verlag, 1989) p. 206.

16 The experience is described in Brian Richardson 'Architecture for All' *The Raven* Vol. 2 No. 2, October 1988, pp. 146-154, and in a forthcoming book on Self-Build by Brian Richardson and Jon Broome to be published by Green Books.

17 Ken Atkins cited by Colin Ward *When We Build Again* (Pluto Press, 1985) p. 71.

18 Walter Segal 'View from a lifetime' *Transactions of the RIBA* Vol. I, 1982, pp. 7-14.

7 · THE HAMMERSMITH GUEST HOUSE AGAIN

1 The Society for the Protection of Ancient Buildings, founded in April 1877. Included amongst the original membership were Carlyle, Ruskin, Webb, Faulkner, Holman Hunt and Burne-Jones.

2 J.W. Mackail *The Life of William Morris* 2 vols (1899). Reprint edn., (London: Benjamin Blom, 1968) Vol I, p. 233.

3 Morris was articled to the architect G.E. Street but, on the encouragement of Rosetti, gave up architecture in favour of painting after less than a year.

4 See Nikolaus Pevsner, *Pioneers of Modern Design* (London: Faber & Faber, 1936) and also Rayner Banham, *Theory and Design in the First Machine Age* (London: Architectural Press, 1962).

5 *N.F.N.*, p. 187.

6 Ibid., pp. 187-8.

7 Ray Watkinson, Foreword to *The Politics of Architecture* by John Hanna (London: William Morris Society, 1983).

8 John Hanna, *The Politics of Architecture* (London: William Morris Society, 1983).

9 Le Corbusier, *Towards a New Architecture* (London: Faber, 1927).

10 See Manfredo Tafuri, *Architecture and Utopia* trans. Barbara Luigia La Penta (Cambridge, Mass.: the MIT Press, 1976) p. 100 for a criticism of Le Corbusier's 'quietist' position from a Marxist viewpoint.

11 See, for instance, Henry van de Velde's 'Credo' of 1907 in *Programmes and Manifestos on 20th-century Architecture*, ed. Ulrich Conrads (London: Lund Humphries, 1970) p. 18

12 See David Watkin *Morality and Architecture* (Oxford: Clarendon Press, 1977) for a comprehensive (but right-wing) account of this debate.

13 See Nikolaus Pevsner, *Studies in Art, Architecture and Design: Victorian and After* (1968, reprinted, Princeton: Princeton University Press, 1982) for confirmation of Morris's ambiguous relationship to architects and designers ('squinters on paper'). Pevsner makes the important observation that Morris never publicly proclaimed Webb as his architectural champion.

This corresponds exactly with Ruskin's affirmation in the preface to the second edition of *The Seven Lamps of Architecture* (1855): 'The fact is, there are only two fine arts possible to the human race, sculpture and painting. What we call architecture is only the association of these in noble masses, or the placing of them in fit places.'

14 *N.F.N.*, p. 363.

15 Bernard Rudofsky, *Architecture without Architects* (London: Academy Editions, 1964).

16 'The Stones of Venice II' (1853) in Ruskin *Works* 10, p. 188.

17 Margaret Richardson, *Architects of the Arts and Crafts Movement* (London: Trefoil Books Ltd., 1983) p.16.

18 *N.F.N.*, p. 362.

19 Ibid., p. 363.

20 Ibid., p. 192.

21 J. Hanna, op. cit. pp. 38-39.

22 E.P. Thompson, *William Morris: Romantic to Revolutionary* (New York: Pantheon Books, 1955) p. 686.

23 *N.F.N.*, p. 202. It is interesting to note that the extension to 'Red House' at Bexleyheath, planned in 1864 but not executed, was conceived in a different style from the existing building. Peter Blundell Jones, in his excellent article in the *Architects Journal*, (15th January, 1986) attributes the change of material (from red brick to tile hanging and timber frame) either to Webb's improved knowledge of the Kentish vernacular or to a desire that the idea

of 'extension' should be made manifest. See also George Devey's work at Penshurst Place as an example of mid-Victorian eclectic and accretive compositional tactics.

24 Demetri Porphyrios, *Sources of Modern Eclecticism* (London: Academy Editions, 1982) p. 68.

25 *N.F.N.*, p. 391.

26 W. R. Lethaby, *Philip Webb and his Work* (Oxford: O.U.P., 1935; reprinted, London: Raven Oak Press, 1979) p. 128.

27 But see Porphyrios' argument for Alvar Aalto's typological approach in Demetri Porphyrios, *Sources of Modern Eclecticism* (London: Academy Editions, 1982) pp. 25-39.

28 See Manfredo Tafuri, *Architecture and Utopia*, op. cit. 'Architecture as ideology of the plan is swept away by the reality of the plan when, the level of utopia having been superseded, the plan becomes an operative mechanism.'

29 E. P. Thompson, *William Morris: Romantic to Revolutionary* (New York: Pantheon Books, 1955) p. 686.

30 The details of More's proposals are extracted from Ian Tod and Michael Wheeler, *Utopia* (London: Orbis Publishing, 1978) pp. 29-34.

8 · A MARKET BY THE WAY

1 Thomas More *Utopia* (1551) English translation by Ralph Robinson (London).

2 K. Marx & F. Engels *Manifesto of the Communist Party (1848)*.

3 *N.F.N.*, p. 288.

4 W. Morris 'Communism' in A. L. Morton, ed. *Political Writings of William Morris* (Lawrence & Wishart, 1973) pp. 234-245.

5 *N.F.N.*, p. 368.

6 P. Meier An unpublished lecture of William Morris: 'How shall we live then?', *International Review of Social History* XVI (2) (1971) pp. 1-24.

7 *N.F.N.*, pp. 188-9.

8 Ibid., p. 217.

9 Ibid., p. 213.
10 E. Cabet *Oeuvres d'Etienne Cabet*, Tome 1 (Paris: Anthropon, 1970).
11 E. Bellamy *Looking Backward* (1889) republished by Harmondsworth (1986).
12 'How we live, and how we might live' in A.L. Morton op. cit.
13 *N.F.N.* p. 257.
14 W. Morris & E.B. Bax *Socialism, Its Growth and Outcome* (London: 1893) pp. 213 & 219.
15 See note 6.
16 *N.F.N.*, p. 270.
17 Ibid.
18 'The Dawn of a New Epoch' in W. Morris *Signs of Change* (London: 1888) p. 199.
19 W. Morris & E.B. Bax, op. cit., p. 220.
20 Ibid., p. 219.
21 P. Meier *La Pensée Utopique de William Morris* 2 vols (Paris: (1972).
22 *N.F.N.*, pp. 276-7.
23 Ibid., p. 280.
24 C. Ward, ed. *Peter Kropotkin—Fields, Factories, Workshops—Tomorrow!* (George Allen & Unwin, 1974).
25 M. Bookchin 'Towards a liberatory technology' in *Post-Scarcity Anarchism* (Berkeley, California: Ramparts Press). See also 'Towards an ecological society' in M. Bookchin *Towards an Ecological Society* (Montreal, Canada: Black Rose Books, 1981).
26 N. Thompson *The Market and its Critics* (Routledge, 1988).
27 *N.F.N.*, p. 250.
28 Ibid., p. 226.
29 Ibid., p. 350.
30 A. Nove *Feasible Socialism* (George Allen & Unwin, 1983).
31 Ibid.
32 *N.F.N.*, p. 267.
33 Ibid., p. 366.
34 H. Daly, ed. *Towards a Steady State Economy* (Freeman, 1973).

9 · THE ENDING OF THE JOURNEY

1 N. Gould 'William Morris', *Ecologist* 4 (1974) pp. 210-212.

2 E.P. Thompson *William Morris: Romantic to Revolutionary* (Merlin, 1976, second edition).

3 A. Briggs, ed. *William Morris: News from Nowhere, and selected writings and designs* (Penguin, 1984). See also A.L. Morton, ed. *Political Writings of William Morris* (Lawrence & Wishart, 1984, second edition).

4 Ibid.

5 J. Robertson *The Sane Alternative: a choice of futures* (Cholney, Oxon: J. Robertson, 1983).

6 A. Briggs, ed., op. cit.

7 From 'The Beauty of Life' (1880) quoted in G. Naylor, ed. *William Morris by himself* (Macdonald Orbis, 1988).

8 In reasoning thus, Morris was surely on to something fundamental. It is nowadays fashionable in some circles to believe that in the future, as computers 'take over' (note the overtones of Bellamy), we shall need increased 'education for leisure'. I have always been deeply suspicious of such ideas, and once I had read *Useful Work* . . . I finally understood why. We can't *all* end up selling each other tickets!

9 J. Robertson op. cit.

10 A. Briggs, ed., op. cit.

11 C. Ward, ed. *Peter Kropotkin—Fields, Factories, Workshops—Tomorrow!* (George Allen & Unwin, (1974).

12 H. Henderson 'The Warp and the Weft: the coming synthesis of ecophilosophy and ecofeminism', in L. Caldecott & S. Leland (eds) *Reclaim the Earth: Women speak out for Life on Earth* (The Women's Press, 1983).

13 J. Robertson, op. cit.

14 W. & D. Schwarz *Breaking Through* (Green Books, 1988).

15 E.P. Thompson op. cit.

16 *N.F.N.*, pp. 254 & 273-282.

17 Ibid., p. 254.

18 Ibid., p. 350.

19 M. Harris *Culture, People, Nature: an Introduction to General Anthropology* (Crowell, 1980).

20 *N.F.N.*, pp. 213-221.

21 M. Sahlins *Stone Age Economics* (Freeman, 1972).

22 D. Pepper 'The Geography of an Anarchist Britain', *The Raven* 1 (4) (1988) pp. 339-350. (An interesting article, but why the *geography* for goodness' sake?!)

23 Perhaps not such a radical change of use after all.

24 *N.F.N.* pp. 254-256.

25 Ibid., pp. 184-186. It is, of course nowadays suggested that the return of salmon to the Thames is a sign that improvements in water quality in that river have taken place. To a certain extent this is true, but all that has really happened is that the once prevalent organic wastes, which demanded high levels of oxygen in the water (hence the disappearance in Victorian times of the salmon), are now more efficiently broken down by treatment into their constituent nutrients. This is not always entirely beneficial, as witnessed by severe problems with algal blooms in rivers, lakes and reservoirs in Britain in the summer of 1989.

26 H. Henderson op. cit.

27 D. Pepper op. cit.

28 J. Robertson op. cit.

29 T. O'Riordan *Environmentalism* (Pion Press, 1981, second edition). The terminology used here, however, is from his article 'Future directions for environmental policy' in *Environment and Planning* A, 17, pp. 1431-1446.

30 See also P. E. O'Sullivan, *International Journal of Environmental Studies* 28, pp. 257-267 (1987).

31 E. F. Schumacher *Small is Beautiful—a study of economics as if people mattered* (Blond & Briggs, 1973).

32 After J. Lovelock *Gaia: a new look at Life on Earth* (Cambridge University Press, 1979).

33 For a summary see B. Devall & G. Sessions *Deep Ecology: living as if Nature mattered* (Peregrine Smith, 1983).

34 'O me! O me! How I love the Earth and the seasons, and weather, and all things that deal with it, and all that grows out of it . . .' *N.F.N.* p. 391.

35 See M. Bookchin (1987) 'Social Ecology versus Deep Ecology—a challenge for the Ecology movement', *The Raven* 1 (3), pp. 219-250.

36 D. Morrison 'The soft, cutting edge of environmentalism. How and why the Appropriate Technology notion is changing the movement', *Natural Resources Journal* 20 (1980) pp. 275-298.

37 C. Thomas 'Alternative Technology : a Feminist Technology?', in L. Caldecott & S. Leland eds (1983) op. cit.

38 H. Daly, ed. *Towards a Steady State Economy* (Freeman 1973).

39 K. Boulding 'The Shadow of the Stationary State', *Daedalus* 109 (1973) pp. 89-102.

ᨠ BIBLIOGRAPHY ᨢ

A NOTE ON FURTHER READING

There are two current English editions of *News from Nowhere*. These are published by Routledge and Kegan Paul (London: 1970), with an introduction by James Redmond, and by Lawrence & Wishart (London: 1968), with an introduction by A.L. Morton. The latter, entitled *Three Works by William Morris* also contains the full text of *A Dream of John Ball*, and *The Pilgrims of Hope*, and is the version to which we have made page reference in all notes throughout this book.

There is an abridged version of the novel in the book edited by Asa Briggs listed below, but we do not recommend reading a partial version of Morris's vision. There are no books which deal specifically with *News from Nowhere*, but many of those listed below, which are on Morris, or on aspects of utopian thought, contain material which we hope will be of interest to readers of the novel.

BIBLIOGRAPHY

Aho, Gary *William Morris—a reference guide* (Boston: 1985).

Aldred, Guy *Pioneers of Antiparliamentarianism.* (Glasgow: 1940).

Anderson, Perry *Arguments within English Marxism.* (London: 1980).

Armytage, W.H.G. *Yesterday's Tomorrow: A Historical Survey of Future Societies* (London: 1968).

Arnot, R. Page *William Morris—A Vindication.* (London: 1934).

Arnot, R. Page *William Morris, The Man and the Myth.* (London: 1964).

Banham, Joanna & Harris, Jennifer *William Morris and the Middle Ages*. (Manchester: 1984).

Bellamy, Edward *Looking Backward* (republished London: 1986).

Berneri, M.L. *Journey Through Utopia*. (London: 1972).

Boos, Florence ed. *William Morris's Socialist Diary* (London: 1985).

Bradley, I. *William Morris and His World* (London: 1978).

Briggs, Asa *William Morris, Selected Writings and Designs* (London 1962). Republished as *William Morris, News from Nowhere, and Selected Writings and Designs*. (London: 1984).

Bulla, G. *William Morris: fra arte e rivoluzione*. (Cassino: 1980).

Calhoun, B. *The Pastoral Vision of William Morris: 'The Earthly Paradise'* (Athens, Georgia: 1975).

Callenbach, E. *Ecotopia* (London: 1978).

Cole, G.D.H. *William Morris as a Socialist* (London: 1960).

Colebrook, F. *William Morris, Master Printer* (Tunbridge Wells: 1897).

Compton-Rickett, A. *William Morris—A Study in Personality* (London: 1913, reprinted 1971).

Crane, Walter *William Morris to Whistler* (London: 1911).

Crow, G.M. *William Morris, Designer* (London: 1934).

Design Council, The *William Morris & Kelmscott* (London: 1981).

Drinkwater, John *William Morris, a Critical Study* (London: 1912).

Faulkner, Peter *William Morris and W.B. Yeats* (Dublin: 1962).

Faulkner, Peter *William Morris and Eric Gill* (London: 1975).

Faulkner, Peter *Against the Age: an Introduction to William Morris*. (London: 1980).

Faulkner, Peter *Wilfrid Scawen Blunt and the Morrises* (London: 1981).

Fitzgerald, P. *The Novel on Blue Paper by William Morris* (London & New York: 1982).

Fritzsche, G. *William Morris' Socialismus und Anarchistischen Kommunismus* (New York: 1967).

Furneaux Jordan, R. *The Medieval Vision of William Morris* (London: 1960).

Gardner, D. *An 'Idle Singer' and his Audience* (The Hague: 1975).

Gaunt, W. *The Pre-Raphaelite Tragedy*. (London: 1942).

Gillow, Norah *William Morris Designs and Patterns* (London: 1988).

Glasier, J. Bruce *William Morris and the Early Days of the Socialist Movement* (London: 1921).

Goodwin, Barbara and Taylor, Keith *The Politics of Utopia* (London: 1982).

Grennan, M.R. *William Morris, Medievalist and Revolutionary* (London: 1945).

Grey, Lloyd Eric *William Morris, Prophet of England's New Order* (London: 1949).

Harrison, Royden *Before the Socialists: Studies in Labour and Politics, 1861-1881.* (London: 1965).

Henderson, Philip ed. *The Letters of William Morris to his Family and Friends* (London: 1950).

Henderson, Philip *William Morris: His Life, Work and Friends* (London: 1967).

Hodson A., *Romances of William Morris* (Cambridge: 1987).

Hough, Graham *The Last Romantics* (London: 1949).

Institute of Contemporary Arts *William Morris Today* (London: 1984).

Jackson, Holbrook *William Morris* (London: 1926, reprinted 1971).

Jackson, Holbrook *William Morris and the Arts and Crafts* (New York: 1934, reprinted Folcroft PA: 1974).

Kelvin, N. ed. *The Collected Letters of William Morris* (3 vols) (Princeton: 1986).

Kirchoff, F. *William Morris (Boston: 1979).*

Kirsch, H.-C. *William Morris—ein Mann gegen Die Zeit: Leben und Werk* (Cologne: 1983).

Kumar, Krishnan *Utopia and Anti-Utopia in Modern Times* (London: 1987).

Leatham, J. *William Morris, Master of Many Crafts* (London: 1980).

Lemire, E.D., ed. *Unpublished Lectures of William Morris* (Detroit: 1969).

Lethaby, W.R. *William Morris as Work-Master* (London: 1901).

Lindsay, Jack *William Morris, His Life and Works* (London: 1975).

Mackail, J.W. *The Life of William Morris (2 vols) (London: 1898).*

Mackail, J.W. *William Morris and his circle* (London: 1907).

Manuel, F.E. and Manuel, F.P. eds. *Utopian Thought in the Western World* (Oxford: 1979).

Marsh, Jan *Pre-Raphaelite Sisterhood* (London: 1985).

Marsh, Jan *Jane and May Morris: a Biographical Story, 1839-1938.* (London: 1986).

Marshall, R. *William Morris and his Earthly Paradises* (London: 1979).

Meier, Paul *Nouvelles de Nulle Part* (Paris: 1961).

Meier, Paul *La Pensée Utopique de William Morris.* (Paris: 1972).

Meier, Paul *William Morris, The Marxist Dreamer* (2 vols) (Brighton: 1978).

Morris, May, ed. *The Collected Works of William Morris* (24 vols) (London: 1910–15).

Morris, May *William Morris, Artist, Writer, Socialist* (2 vols) (Oxford: 1936).

Morton, A.L. *The English Utopia* (London: 1953).

Morton, A.L., ed. *Political Writings of William Morris* (London: 1973).

Naylor, Gillian *The Arts & Crafts Movement: a study of its sources, ideals and influence on Design Theory* (London: 1981).

Naylor, Gillian *William Morris by Himself* (London: 1988).

Noyes, Alfred *William Morris* (London: 1908).

Oberg, Charlotte *A Pagan Prophet: William Morris* (Charlottesville VA: 1978).

Parry, Linda *William Morris Textiles* (London: 1983).

Parry, Linda *William Morris & the Arts and Craft Movement— a source book* (London: 1989).

Pevsner, Nikolaus *Pioneers of the Modern Movement, from William Morris to Walter Gropius* (London: 1936).

Pevsner, Nikolaus *Pioneers of Modern Design* (London: 1986).

Pierson S. *Marxism, and the Origins of British Socialism* (Cornell: 1972).

Poulson, Christine *William Morris* (London: 1989).

Rubel, Maximilien and Crump, John *Non-Market Socialism in the Nineteenth and Twentieth Centuries* (London: 1987).

Silver, Carole *The Romance of William Morris* (Athens, Ohio: 1982).

Simon, Roger *William Morris Now* (London: 1984).

Sparling, H. Halliday *The Kelmscott Press and William Morris, Master Craftsman* (London: 1924).

Stansky, P. *William Morris* (Oxford: 1983).

Swannell, J.N. *William Morris and Old Norse Literature* (London: 1961).

Tames, R. *William Morris—an Illustrated Life* (Princes Risborough, Bucks, UK: 1972).

Thomas, H. *A Visit to William Morris* (Andoversford: 1979).

Thompson, E.P. *William Morris, Romantic to Revolutionary* (London: 1977).

Thompson, Paul *The Work of William Morris* (London: 1967).

Tsuzuki, C. H. M. *Hyndman and British Socialism* (Oxford: 1961).

Vallance, Aymer *William Morris: His Art, His Writings and His Public Life* (London: 1897). (Republished in facsimile, London: 1986).

Wahl, J.R. *No Idle Singer* (Cape Town: 1964).

Wandel, R. *Socialkritik und regressive Ideale in den politisch engagierten Schriften von William Morris* (Frankfurt: 1981).

Ward, Colin ed. *Peter Kropotkin—Fields, Factories, Workshops—Tomorrow!* (London: 1979).

Watkinson, Ray *William Morris as Designer* (London: 1967).

Wiles, H.V. *William Morris of Walthamstow* (London: 1951).

Williams, Raymond *Culture and Society, 1780-1950* (London: 1959).

Woodcock, George *Anarchism—a history of libertarian ideas* (London: 1962).

❧ BIOGRAPHICAL DETAILS OF CONTRIBUTORS ❧

CHRISTOPHER HAMPTON is Senior Lecturer in English at the Polytechnic of Central London. His publications include *The Etruscans* (Gollancz 1969, Doubleday 1970), *An Exile's Italy* (poems, Thonnesen 1972), *A Cornered Freedom* (poems, Peterloo Poets 1980), *Socialism in a Crippled World* (Penguin 1981), and *A Radical Reader : The Struggle for Change in England, 1381–1914* (Penguin 1984). He has also written scripts for films, television and radio. A new book, *The Ideology of the Text*, on the interaction of literature, politics, and history, is to be published by the Open University Press in June 1990.

JOHN CRUMP was born in Yorkshire in 1944. He is Lecturer in Politics at the University of York, and his publications include *The Origins of Socialist Thought in Japan* (Croom Helm, 1983), *State Capitalism : the Wages System Under New Management*, (with Adam Buick, published by Macmillan, 1986), and *Non-Market Socialism in the Nineteenth and Twentieth Centuries* (Macmillan, 1987, co-edited with Maximilien Rubel.

STEPHEN COLEMAN is Professor of the History of Ideas on the London campus of Drew University, New Jersey. He is author of a biographical work, *Daniel DeLeon* (Manchester University Press, 1989), has written several articles on utopias and utopian thought, including some for *The Journal of the William Morris Society*, and is currently working on a book, to be published in 1991/2, on *Utopia and Theories of Human Nature*. He first read *News from Nowhere* when he was fifteen, and it, together with Robert Tressell's *The Ragged-Trousered Philanthropists* made an impact upon his thinking about society which remains undiminished.

RAY WATKINSON is one of the most respected Morris scholars in the world today. He has been editor of *The Journal of the William Morris Society*, and in 1984 was one of the principal contributors to the ICA's exhibition 'William Morris Today', held to mark the 150th anniversary of Morris's birth. He has lectured and written extensively on Morris, and is the author of *William Morris As Designer* (Studio Vista, 1967), which has subsequently been republished in several languages, including a Japanese edition in 1984. He is currently working on two books, including one on Ford Maddox Brown.

JAN MARSH is a writer and biographer with a special interest in the women of William Morris's circle in the second half of the nineteenth century. She is author of *Pre-Raphaelite Sisterhood* (1985), *Jane and May Morris* (1986), *Women Artists and the Pre-Raphaelite Movement* (with Pamela Gerrish Nunn, 1989), *The Legend of Elizabeth Siddal* (1989), and television documentaries on the Arts and Crafts Movement, and May Morris. She is currently working on the representation of race in Victorian art.

COLIN WARD is a writer whose books tend to explore popular and unofficial uses of the environment. They include *Arcadia for All*, and *Goodnight Campers* (both written with Dennis Hardy), and *The Allotment* (with David Crouch), as well as his well-known books *Anarchy in Action*, *The Child in The City*, and *The Child in The Country*. The most recent is *Welcome Thinner City* (Bedford Square Press).

MARK PEARSON is 29, and trained as an architect. He has collaborated on various building projects with architectural practices in London and the Southwest, but has wider interests in design and making, with woodwork being his first love. His more polemical architectural drawings have appeared in exhibitions in London and Plymouth, and have been published in *Building Design*, and *Architect's Journal*. He now lives in Devon, having recently taken a post as Senior Lecturer in the School of Architecture, Polytechnic South West. He is a member of the SPAB, the William Morris Society, and has a particular enthusiasm for prehistoric archaeological sites.

ADAM BUICK has worked for a financial newspaper, a trade union, and as an international civil servant. He has written extensively on socialism and state capitalism (including, with John Crump, *State Capitalism : the Wages System under New Management*, Macmillan, 1986), and on economics and ecology.

PADDY O'SULLIVAN is Senior Lecturer in Environmental Science at Polytechnic South West. Like many people, he became interested in Morris during the 1960s, when the designs came back into vogue, but it was not until late in the 70s that he fully realized that Morris had arrived at the concept of an ecological society long before anyone else had heard of the term. He now teaches both environmental philosophy and Environmental Science at Polytechnic South West, and researches into the ways in which Nature has recorded human impact by storing information in the sediments at the bottom of lakes and ponds. His long-term project is the development of the truly 'green' science which Morris first described in 1877!

ILLIAM MORRIS SOCIETY
President ✥ Lord Briggs of Lewes
Honorary Secretary ✍ R. S. Smith
Kelmscott House, 26 Upper Mall,
Hammersmith, London W6 9TA

The purpose of the William Morris Society is to make the life, work and ideas of William Morris better known in the world of today.

The many-sidedness of Morris, and the variety of activities in which he engaged bring together in the Society those who are interested in him as a poet, designer, craftsman, printer, pioneer socialist, dreamer, or who admire his robust and generous personality, his extraordinary vitality, his creative concentration and his courage. Morris aimed for a state of affairs in which all might enjoy the potential richness of human life. He provides a focus for those who deplore the progressive dehumanisation of the world in the twentieth century, and who believe, with him, that the trend is not inevitable.

The Society provides up-to-date information on topics of interest to its members, arranges talks, meetings, exhibitions and visits, encourages republication of his works and the continued manufacture of his textile and wallpaper designs, and itself publishes commentaries on and studies of particular aspects of his work and of his achievement in general. Members of the Society receive *The Journal* twice a year.

For full details of the William Morris Society, apply to:

The Hon. Secretary, William Morris Society, Kelmscott House, 26 Upper Mall, Hammersmith, London W6 9TA.